Preface

Although children's books have long enjoyed a privileged place in Unesco's book development efforts, the International Year of the Child (1979) has given new impetus and meaning to these efforts, focusing worldwide attention on the importance of children's literature in shaping individuals who are at the same time comfortably rooted in their cultural past and well equipped to confront the increasing complexity of contemporary life.

Nowhere is this more keenly understood than in the developing countries. But despite the increasing emphasis on providing free compulsory education to growing numbers of children, a broad gap remains between expanding educational commitments and the resources available to support and sustain these endeavours. Low literacy levels, high production costs, poor purchasing power, disorganized and often linguistically fragmented markets, inadequate professional training, lack of materials and equipment—the obstacles to children's book production are pronounced and manifold. Yet it has been observed, time and time again, that no programme of formal education, however broad and well organized, can have lasting effect if sufficient supplementary reading material is not available to maintain interest, improve skills and encourage children to begin an intimate, lifelong friendship with the printed word.

The present publication, as part of Unesco's efforts within the framework of IYC, seeks to draw attention to the specific factors which hamper the spread of children's books in developing countries. After a brief survey of the growth of children's literature as a separate and distinct publishing phenomenon, the author examines each element in the creative process, exploring both historical context and current situation so as to present a detailed description of the host of problems which must be resolved if 'the book hunger' of the majority of the world's children is to be appeased. By breaking down into its component parts the seemingly massive and tangled issue of 'children's books in developing countries', the author is then able to tackle each question in turn, broadening her definition to include all forms of reading matter that appeal to children and that spring from local customs and tradition so as to provide ideas and suggestions for countries at all levels of publishing capacity.

Anne Pellowski is in a unique position to do so. As a recognized authority on international literature and non-print media for children, she created and directs the Information Center on Children's Cultures of the United States Committee for Unicef. This combination library-museum-classroom is considered one of the most important repositories in the United States of primary source materials on the cultures of children in developing countries and is a major reference point for educators, publishers, film-makers, writers and illustrators.

A former story-teller and specialist in public library group work, Miss Pellowski has travelled extensively, studying and teaching in Africa, Asia, Europe and Latin America. She is an active member of the International Board on Books for Young People (IBBY) and the American Library Association, which presented her with its 1979 Grolier Foundation Award. Her publications include *The World of Storytelling* (R. R. Bowker), and she has recorded a story-telling series on international folklore.

This book is thus the fruit of the author's long personal experience with children's literature around the world. While in no way exhaustive, it can serve as a useful springboard for devising comprehensive, integrated approaches to planning children's book industries throughout the developing world. Although the author's views do not necessarily reflect those of Unesco, the Organization considers this book both timely and thought-provoking.

MADE
TO MEASURE:
CHILDREN'S BOOKS
IN DEVELOPING
COUNTRIES

Anne Pellowski

unesco

Published in 1980
by the United Nations Educational,
Scientific and Cultural Organization,
7 place de Fontenoy, 75700 Paris
Printed by Imprimerie des Presses Universitaires de France,
Vendôme

ISBN 92–3–101783–7
French edition: 92–3–201783–0
Spanish edition: 92–3–301783–4

Contents

Contents

Foreword

This book is the result of some twenty-five years of experience observing how children respond to books and stories of all types and to various printed, visual and oral forms of stories. Furthermore, this opportunity to work with and observe children took place in rural and village areas, urban and suburban areas, in institutions, in groups, with individuals, and in quite a number of countries.

An acquaintance of mine, who once watched Norman Borlaug, the father of the Green Revolution, as he sized up a new field of rice growing in a country and area he had not visited previously, remarked on the amazing rapidity with which he could tell most of the particulars about that rice field: exact type of rice being grown, soil content, number of days of growth, amount it would yield, etc.

Observing children and coming to such swift conclusions is a bit more difficult. There are, of course, certain physical characteristics that stand out immediately, and the greater number and variety of children one has seen, the more likely one is to be right about their age and general health. But judging such elusive and hard-to-define areas as intellectual growth, aesthetic response, imaginative engagement or humorous involvement can be very erratic. One is apt to be completely wrong in one's conclusions, and not necessarily just because of language or cultural barriers. Children are after all individuals, even though adults often like to lump them into convenient and homogeneous groups.

The results of my observations are not to be taken as absolute, since I have inevitably seen and reported things in ways that appear objective to me but that surely contain a good deal of the subjective, and perhaps even of the biased. I can only state that when I have come to some of the more general conclusions that seem applicable to a wide variety of children, it has been as a result of verifying first-hand observations with as much research data as I can find, especially data compiled by others. I have also tried to consult, listen to and read the theories of many persons who also work with children and books, pictures and stories. The specific questions posed in this book were addressed by mail to a number of children's literature experts throughout the world. In addition, several respondents provided articles or papers and authorized the use of selected segments.

So many other persons have given me ideas and inspiration that it is impossible to cite all of them here. I have tried to include the specific points of view of as many as possible. No doubt I have left out many important perspectives. Those who have had experience with children, books and reading are encouraged to send me their comments, but in particular I would like to hear from persons in economically developing nations who have different or expanded views from those cited in this book.

ACKNOWLEDGEMENTS

This book was written with the assistance of Dr Julinda Abu Nasr, Professor of Child Development, Beirut University College, Lebanon; Meshack Asare, illustrator, Ghana Publishing Corporation, Ghana; Gian Calvi, illustrator and graphic designer, Brazil; Marilyn Hirsh, illustrator, United States, with experience in India; Manorama Jafa, Convener, Writers' Workshop, Children's Book Trust, India; Dr Ayşe Kudat, Development Foundation of Turkey; Molly Melching, Peace Corps volunteer and Co-director of the Tostan Library and Cultural Centre for Children maintained by the Centre Culturel Africain, Ministry of Culture, Senegal; Mrs Touran Mirhadi, critic and educator, Iran; Paul N. Njoroge, Editorial

Department, East African Publishing House, Kenya; Aisake
M. Raratabu, managing director, Lotu Pasifika Productions
(LPP), Fiji; Mabel D. Segun, author and the president of
the Children's Literature Association of Nigeria; C. D. Shah,
general manager, Text Book Centre Limited, Kenya; Veronica
Uribe, editor, Ediciones Ekaré-Banco del Libro, Venezuela;
and Margarita Francia Villaluz, author and the president of
the Philippine Writers' Guild on Children's Literature.

PART I

A brief history
of children's literature

Historically, books for children have fallen into three main types:

Type 1: religious-moral-social tracts. These were the earliest type, and were meant principally for use with individual children. They were intended to be introduced by parents, tutors, religious leaders or social mentors. They were not usually designed for use with classroom groups. This type is still common in some societies, especially those in which religious or moral teaching is carried out in the home environment. Occasionally, they are made to be partly entertaining to enhance appeal.

Type 2: textbooks and supplementary classroom books. These often have selections or segments similar to the above type of book, but they are usually designed for use in schoolroom groups using formal and prescribed steps, under the guidance of a teacher. In other words, their success is mostly determined by how effective they are with large numbers of children using them simultaneously. In some countries, the contents are selected from adult literature; in others they are specifically written with children in mind; in still others, the two types of literature are combined. In the twentieth century, a movement began in the United States of America to control the vocabulary of this type of book according to various formulae arrived at by educators who studied verbal and reading patterns of children at different levels. This had a wide influence on American textbooks and textbooks in countries that used American models. More recently, the trend has been to select already existing texts and to rate them according to readability formulae that involve such factors as length and difficulty of vocabulary, sentences and paragraphs; active and passive modes; direct or indirect dialogue; complexity of concepts, etc. Rather than having writers compose texts to order, then, the textbook editor selects those already written and considered suitable for the particular subject and level. In this manner, quite a number of pieces of children's literature have found their way into textbooks.

Type 3: recreational and informational books. (a) Trade books are those edited, designed and published by trade publishers for sale through jobbers and book stores. They are concerned with all subject matter, and also include such forms as picture story books, biographies, novels, poetry, drama and episodic fiction for children. They are only rarely written and illustrated by persons on the staff of the publishing house. (b) The category of mass-market books includes all books edited, designed and published for sale through mass-media outlets such as corner news-stands, supermarkets, chains of variety stores and any other similar outlets. In order to be commercially viable for these types of sales outlet, the books are designed in series formats, i.e. all books in a given series have the same physical size so that they fit into the racks designed to sell them as fast as they come out. Some of these books are written and illustrated by individual authors, and others are composed by groups of staff writers paid to write and design to a specific style. They often include the same characters, placed in different situations. A major sub-type of this mass market book is the comic book. Although its format has also been occasionally used for tract books and textbooks, it falls chiefly in the recreational area. The same can be said for children's magazines.

This book will deal only with the last two types mentioned, with the main emphasis on recreational and informational books, Type 3.

Most developing countries have had at least a few books of Type 1, either entirely locally inspired, or subsidized and inspired by outside missionary groups seeking to spread their message. In some cases, the only local printing and publishing facilities available are the direct result of the desire to publish religious tracts and stories in local vernaculars. Their influence on the general field of children's book publishing should not be overlooked.

Textbooks that are written, designed, printed and published locally are still a rarity in quite a number of countries. They are either directly published by government units or by autonomous agencies set up by government. An example of the former would be the publications of the Ministry of Education in Thailand; examples of the latter can be found in the Comisión Nacional de Libros de Textos Gratuitos in Mexico and in the Janak Education Materials Centre in Nepal. In some countries, texts are published by commercial firms, which then must submit them for approval by appropriate units in government. In some cases there are 'obligatory' texts as well as 'approved' texts. Other countries select certain textbooks published in some of the major publishing centres of the world (e.g. the United Kingdom, France, Spain, the United States), make some adaptations to fit their needs, and agree with the publishers on the number to be printed for their national use. This has been especially common in certain Latin American countries and in some of the French-speaking African countries.

In many countries, there is often only one approved choice at any given level and in any given subject. For example, all children in fourth-year primary school are likely to be using the same reading, mathematics, social sciences and sciences texts in all parts of the country, even though they might be in different languages.

The chief advantages of this are that (a) costs can be kept as low as possible, (b) government authorities can feel assured that the same basic material is being covered in all schools, and (c) children can identify with each other on a national level, even though they may have local or regional differences in language, social life, customs, etc.

The disadvantages of national uniformity of textbooks are (a) that the uniformity tends to stifle the creative, imaginative impulses of children, who mature intellectually (as well as physically) at different rates of speed; and (b) that the books tend to be boring, because in trying to please all, and offend none, they develop a blandness of style that is overpowering.

There have been numerous surveys on the extent and quality of textbooks in developing countries, so this type of children's book publishing will be given much less attention here. Those wishing to learn more about the specifics of the subject can consult the items mentioned in the bibliography.

Recreational books for children are the type least likely to be encountered in developing countries. It is in this area that the experience of economically developed countries has differed greatly. For the most part, in Europe, North America and Japan, children's books of Type 1 gave way to those of Type 3, and only later did the standardized textbook for children come into being. Mass-market and trade books for children began to be common in the early nineteenth century. They had been preceded by picture sheets, chap-books, battledores (a three-leaved folded cardboard format), penny 'theatres' and a host of other formats intended for the adult and general audience as much as for children. These formats were generally very accessible to children because they were cheap, visually easy to read, and on popular subjects. Methods of marketing included fixed stalls and stores, but more often than not travelling vendors sold outdoors at weekly markets that drew crowds of sufficient numbers to support sales of their latest instalments; some sold from door to door. People did not have to be fully literate to be enticed into buying many of the materials, since they were so often visual.

The process of passing from the itinerant story-teller to one who sold essentially the same kinds of 'stories' but in print or visual formats has not occurred in many developing countries. Simple hand or mechanical processes of printing were not nearly the stumbling blocks they have been made out to be, but the lack of inexpensive, readily available paper was and still is certainly one of the major reasons for lack of development of this type of material.

Children in developing countries rarely have enough pocket money to choose what they will buy for themselves, nor can they decide what will be bought for them out of the total expendable income available to the family. When they do have pocket money to spend, it is usually not enough to buy a book, except in those few cases where mass marketing has penetrated sufficiently to bring the sales price to the lowest possible levels. Parents and other adults, on the other hand, are not yet convinced of the need for buying books for their children. If they do buy them, the books tend to be the overly didactic type that parents believe are good for their children's education. The 'uses' of the enchantment of printed literature for children are not clear to the average parent, not even in places where oral story-telling is still considered a good thing. They see no reason to buy books that are 'fun' for their children.

Another obstacle to the development of locally produced children's books has been the ease with which books, especially children's books, can be imported in many areas of the world. Let us hasten to state that the free flow of books is of vital interest to all parts of the world, and should not be impeded. Nevertheless, competition from giant printing and publishing empires, with their huge multilingual, full-colour printings at low cost, has often stifled local production. The international development agencies have been slow to recognize this problem. The answer is not to prevent the entry of such materials into the country (as some have threatened to do) but to develop the capacity to produce competitively priced local materials that are more appealing because their content is more satisfying to local children.

In spite of all these difficulties, there have been a few developing countries that have produced a substantial amount of children's recreational and informational literature in print format. This refers to both mass-market and trade materials, and includes translated or adapted books. The appearance ranges from very poor to quite good quality. In terms of appeal to and satisfaction of children's needs, the materials range from very poor to a few which are outstanding.

It is virtually impossible to cite accurate statistics on trade, text and mass-market children's book production in developing countries. This is especially true for the earlier years of this century. Even countries with advanced publishing industries do not agree on the definition of what constitutes a 'book'. Unesco has attempted a formula, but it is still not too satisfactory, since the minimum forty-nine-page requirement leaves out most picture books and easy readers for young children.

Examples of books produced in the developing countries in the late nineteenth century and the first half of the twentieth are harder to come by than the early children's books of Europe and North America. Nor has there been much improvement in acquisition of such items by research libraries since 1950. Therefore, it is difficult to cite good examples that indicate certain trends and progress in improving quality. Included in the present work are reproductions of pages from a selected number chosen mostly because of their ready availability in the Information Center on Children's Cultures. They were also selected to show a variety of approaches to the publishing of children's books for various interest and reading levels.

PART II

PART II

Testing

QUESTIONS

How are written and visual forms of literature tested with children prior to producing children's books? Are there serious differences between spoken and written language, causing lack of understanding on the part of children? Should and can oral literature play a role in the lives of present-day children?

HISTORICAL PERSPECTIVES

Oral narrative was formerly more often in poetry than in prose, probably because rhythm, metre and other aspects of verse made the content easier to remember. In some parts of the world it was actually sung or chanted, rather than recited. However, short prose narrative tales were also told from very early times, and often these were the type familiar to children. Some anthropologists and folklorists dispute that there was an oral literature especially created for and used with children. In their view, these tales were created by and for adults, and later were 'watered down' or 'condensed' into versions with more appeal to children. This certainly did happen to some tales, but considerable evidence supports the theory that a body of tales existed strictly associated with children, having been composed for them and used exclusively with them. Written literature has developed special forms for children only in relatively recent times.

In most parts of the world, the transition from an oral popular literature to a written one took place (or is taking place) over several centuries. The content was invariably on the same or similar subjects, but the forms were new. Thus the drama, lyric poetry, the short story, the novel and the essay for adult general readers all began to appear while extensive oral literature was still being composed and recited. In some cultures, a written literature has been used for centuries by a small, educated minority, existing alongside an oral literature used chiefly by those who cannot read and write.

For children, didactic or moral treatises and fables were the only forms written down in the early centuries of manuscript and printed literature, both in the Eastern as well as the Western Hemisphere. While there is fairly substantial historical evidence to show that children were told entertaining stories, or allowed to listen to those told to adults, they were not given any to read for a long time. The children's fantasy novel, picture story-book, nonsense poetry, modern anthropomorphic animal tale: all are only about a hundred years old as literary forms especially written for children. Reading was a serious business, taught only to a select few. But while the base number of children who are taught to read has increased greatly, the concept of strictly didactic content has not changed much when considered on a world-wide basis. Parents and teachers still look to the didactic, practical side of reading far more than they do to the entertaining, imaginatively liberating aspect.

Testing has usually involved what children are able to read, rather than what they wish to read. Word lists, grammatical structures, 'classical' or purely literary language, the objective, explicit content as contrasted with subjective interpretations—all these are the basis of many evaluative reading tests on which the entire reading programme of a country is often founded. This is perhaps the only reasonable course, given the difficulty of testing for such intangibles as imaginative development, or the transference of fantasy and curiosity into scientific inquiry.

Informal testing by observation is more common, especially in countries with a fairly extensive amount and variety of children's literature in print. The public library for children has been in some cases an ideal place to test the relative merits of certain types of children's book, since there is less pressure there to conform to formal educational demands. However, only a few public libraries have included mass-market materials in their collections, so the data on their appeal and effect (as contrasted with trade children's books and textbooks), when they are available as part of a range of materials, are not yet very extensive.

Testing or observation in the home is probably practised fairly widely on an informal basis, but since it is rarely recorded in a consistent manner, it is extremely difficult to chart the differences in response to literature among children in their homes, and how they can be compared or contrasted with their responses in the school, library or other institution.

In languages with a wide disparity between oral and written style (e.g. Arabic), objective testing has rarely been used to determine the extent of the child's understanding or enjoyment of reading material of a non-didactic nature or even of a purely practical, informational nature. Informal testing through observation of spontaneous selection and response to children's books has also been difficult in these language areas, because there are not enough materials of the non-didactic type available to large groups of children, and few persons are trained in such observation skills. Also, there are few institutions of a non-didactic nature in which to conduct such experimental work.

Another language problem stems from the fact that in many areas of the world, few books are available in local languages, and children consequently do not learn to associate their spoken home language with books and reading. Instead, the very act of reading is associated with something foreign, as is the imposed second language. Virtually all research in this area points towards the conclusion that only the most highly motivated children will absorb, accept and perform well in a second language that is learned principally through writing and reading, especially when the form and the content of the reading seem to have little connection either with practical everyday life or with the imaginative life that corresponds

Made to measure: children's books in developing countries

to the child's. When the home language is not learned in its written and printed forms, the motivation must be doubly powerful for the child to learn to read well.

In recent years there has been a cry for more locally relevant modern content in children's reading materials, especially textbooks. There has also been a movement calling for inclusion in formal education of more content related to local cultural history. But seldom is there any testing of the forms of these materials as they are used in the schools and as they relate (or do not relate) to the earlier oral forms. A good example of this may be found in certain African nations. In the earlier period of purely oral literature, language was often taught by complex forms of 'riddling' that concentrated on ever more difficult patterns of construction, abstract use of language, and many-layered levels of meaning. This writer has yet to see a single language textbook from Africa incorporating this traditional method of learning through entertaining. The same is true of many types of oral African folk-tale that are not told in a straightforward linear manner, but are interrupted with chants, songs, refrains, dances, miming or the like. These folk-tales, when they are put down in written form and used in reading textbooks, are invariably 'translated' into the European style of folk-tale, and use the controlled vocabulary concept common to American textbooks. The reading-text series that gives only the bare outlines of the stories or tales, leaving blank the appropriate spaces for songs, chants or refrains to be spontaneously composed by the teacher and students, has yet to appear.

PRESENT-DAY OUTLOOK

How do you test your material with children?

Asare, Ghana: The only way I have been able to get children's reactions has been to show them my works in the classroom and ask their opinion about them. It has not been quite the formal approach, but spontaneous comments from children on seeing my work in books have often increased my own awareness of how young people see and like to see themselves, as well as how they relate to their environment.

This is why I think there must be some credibility in whatever is written for young people, whether realistic or fantasy. I think illustrations and books generally must strive to usher young people into a more conscious awareness of the world before they try to impose adult fantasy on them. Also, I think that stories and particularly illustrations must help young people to develop good artistic taste, and I believe their own ideas and reactions count in this process.

Melching, Senegal: Books from different countries are needed as examples of what can be done in the area of children's literature. The culturally relevant books we receive at the Centre d'Étude des Civilisations are translated into Wolof by interested Senegalese students for a modest fee. Then, during story hours at the centre, these books are read to groups of children. The children's reaction is noted for each story. In this way, we are able to advise story-writers and illustrators of the types of book that work and those that don't, discussing reasons why. I am now working with young women in the neighbourhood who read to the children. This year the Institut National des Arts plans to send drama students to the centre to do story-telling.

If we find that some books are particularly successful with the children, we will indicate these books to librarians, educators, animators in rural centres, etc., providing them with the publisher's address and translations of the stories.

However, we want mainly to encourage the development of new materials. To this end, groups of children who come to the centre may be used by writers and artists in order to test their materials before they are published. Also, the centre will gather traditional stories that could be simplified and illustrated for book form.

Mirhadi, Iran: The creation of authentic children's literature in Iran, as elsewhere in the world, differs from the preparation of reading material. It needs writers of great capacity and with

Made to measure: children's books in developing countries

a deep understanding of children. The inner evolution of these writers, their own relationship with children, the way they test and study the children's reaction to their works, and also their sources of inspiration present a variety of original aspects.

For the creative writer there is no predetermined or prescribed formula. It is after the publication of a work that the study of children's reactions—by the authors themselves, by librarians and teachers, by critics—becomes meaningful. In this respect much work has been and is to be done in Iran in order to have sound and positive interaction.

An author of more than twenty adaptations of classics in Persian literature, Mehdi Azaryazdi, is a most timid, uncommunicative person; he has hardly any formal education in literature, lives with his elderly mother, and has very little direct contact with children. He has been a toiler all his life, and his books are accepted by children and appear in new printings every year.

Nader Ehrahimi, another creative author, lives and works among children. His observations, his discussions with children, together with his social and educational attitudes and views, are the basis of his stories. He reads his manuscripts to children and has discussions with them.

Mahmood Kianush, a children's poet, is father of two children, but he has discovered the inner world of childhood through his own poetic self and imagination.

From my experience (book discussion groups, writer-reader conversations, book review sessions with children and young adults, studies of topics of interest, free discussions), I can say that rich, original and authentic stories have always made children go farther in discovering the world of nature, life and human relations. I cannot say who learned more during these sessions—the children or the adults. I think both learned equally.

It is true that all reading material prepared in Iran undergoes different adaptations to levels of understanding, vocabulary and reading skill, to present rules and regulations, to traditional and formal values of the society, and to moral and educational needs and necessities.

Studies of reading interests, although carried out locally,

show that there is not much difference between Iranian children and those of other countries, providing they can read well and books are at their disposal from an early age.

Njoroge, Kenya: Feedback on the use of our books with children comes from schools in the form of demand for story-books to supplement English courses in lower and upper primary classes as well as lower secondary classes. Some of our children's book series ('Primary Science Readers' series and 'Our Nation' series) have been very popular with children—to the extent that the latter has already been 'adopted' by the Kenya Schools Equipment Scheme, which is likely to be making regular orders for distribution in our primary schools. The most definite feedback is therefore the adoption of children's literature to supplement formal education.

Segun, Nigeria: As a writer for children and promoter of literature for children, I test material for children's books on my own children and those of neighbours, friends and relations. This method may appear inadequate because these children are not representative of the country's children, but in actual fact they are representative of those few privileged children who have acquired the reading habit and who possess books—mostly children from middle-class homes whose parents are doctors, engineers, lawyers, teachers and other professionals.

I get feedback from children through school libraries and the children's sections of general libraries—not very many. Since most of the children's books produced in the country are used in schools, feedback can be got from interested teachers and enlightened parents who discuss schoolwork with their children.

I must admit, though, that so far there has been very little feedback from the children themselves, the general pattern being to find out the types of book teachers choose for their classes as supplementary readers.

During school library periods, some teachers make their children fill in questionnaires about books they have read, including whether or not they have enjoyed reading them and

Made to measure: children's books in developing countries

what appealed to them in the books. Unfortunately, no study has been made of this wealth of information hidden in staff-room cupboards, the sole purpose of the questionnaires being to ensure that a child did read some books during the library period. The newly formed Children's Literature Association of Nigeria hopes to make use of the information already collected by teachers as well as future 'feedback'.

Villaluz, Philippines: Before I submit any of my stories to publishers, I try to read the story to my neighbours' children, and then to certain grades in schools (for age-level). I get feedback by immediate reaction from the story that has been read; the children's remarks about characters, situations and themes count a lot. If they repeat incidents or quote 'excerpts' from the story, particularly dialogue, I consider the feedback good. If they react to certain antagonists with comments such as 'I hate that fellow' or 'That man is really bad', that means that one of the characters in my story is really mean.

Another good feedback comes from teachers, whose varied approaches can lead to information on comprehension, applicability to certain age- or grade-levels and other things.

Another way of learning children's interest about subjects and themes is by talking to them. They are more frank than adults, and by going directly to them one can obtain unadulterated reaction. However, persuasion is better than force. Once children have been won over by one's stories, they voluntarily come for more *sans* the teacher's prodding.

Are there serious differences between oral and written language in your area? What role should oral literature play in the lives of present-day children?

Kudat, Turkey: In my view there is relatively little difficulty or conflict between the spoken and the written language. First, the tradition of book writing for children is a rather recent phenomenon, coinciding with the period in Turkey's history when the gap between the two languages is being dramatically reduced. That different dialects are not reflected in the written language should not be viewed as a negative factor. On the contrary, unification of the language has important systematic functions.

That there is still a Kurdish-speaking minority concentrated in eastern Turkey is an important question. However, in practice, children's books do not reach even the urban market in the east, where the population is to a large extent bilingual. It is more the absence of any books and, more important, literacy that should receive priority in approaching the east and particularly the rural sector there.

Mirhadi, Iran: We have several language problems in Iran. The most important are (a) the difference between the oral and written language, (b) the difference between oral language in different districts (even villages have differences in dialects) and (c) the existence of ethnic groups with different languages: Azari in the north-west, Kurdish in the west, Balutch in the south-east, Guilak in the north and Arabic in the south-west.

All children throughout Iran learn written Farsi, which is the language the majority of young readers can understand and enjoy.

For a certain period during the last decade some authors thought of using the oral language in their books and used the oral language of the Tehran district. Facts showed that this could not be read and understood in other parts of the country, and young readers encountered many reading difficulties as each writer used a different spelling. It is also important to know that the oral language is very idiomatic, flexible, with a variety of intonations—all difficult for the young and inexperienced reader to understand.

Written language was strengthened thereafter, and at present only a few works for young adults appear in which the oral language is used for parts of direct speech.

Some authors took up subjects and themes on life in different districts of Iran. They started using local words for objects, tools, activities—expressions that on the whole have helped to enrich and revive the simple but poetic prose in children's books.

Made to measure: children's books in developing countries

Folk-tales, rhymes and riddles are an exception, especially the most well-known ones. The forms of words used in them (direct speech) have been maintained.

Segun, Nigeria: Children who speak a vernacular language at home and learn another language at school do have special difficulties in reading. They find it hard to cultivate the reading habit because they spend so much energy and concentration on deciphering the foreign words in the books instead of enjoying their contents. These children lack reading skills, and this puts them off reading—a real vicious circle.

I do not think they should be given children's books to read in both languages until they have acquired the reading habit in their mother tongue. In other words, in their formative years, from the age of 4 to 12, they should be taught in their mother tongue. At this stage, a foreign language should not be the medium of instruction but should be taught as a second language. This method is being used in a pilot project run by the University of Ife, Ile-Ife. Certain classes in a primary school are taught entirely in Yoruba, while control classes are taught in English. It will be interesting to see the results of this experiment.

I believe it is possible to have children's books in the main languages of Nigeria at a cost that is not prohibitive. A team of translators should be trained to translate good children's books into the four main Nigerian languages—Hausa, Igbo, Yoruba and Efik. Common illustrations should reduce costs. If more children acquire the reading habit through reading books in their mother tongue, print runs would increase dramatically, and this should help to make the cost of books less prohibitive.

Uribe, Venezuela: We think both traditional and modern materials are important when a developing country starts publishing for children because they represent the past and present of its culture. Traditional stories, myths and legends, when published, establish a link between oral tradition and printed materials; and according to our experience in libraries they are excellent in promoting reading.

Villaluz, Philippines: The folk literature in the Philippines is rich, colourful and varied because it comes from a number of ethnic groups and regions. Tales, rhymes, riddles and proverbs enhance the understanding by urban children of their ethnic and rural countrymen. There is no substitute for these. On the other hand, ecology, modern agriculture and advances in science and the arts are best introduced through modern concepts, to awaken interest in and update knowledge about these subjects for both rural and urban children. Hence, oral literature handed down to us by our ancestors is just as important to the present generation as are the stories of modern life and themes. Meeting the literary needs of both the urban and rural children is a big challenge to writers. It requires research, industry, determination and that certain touch of magic—communication.

Folk literature and modern children's stories should, I reiterate, be given equal emphasis in order that today's generation can savour the past and also enjoy the present.

Writing

Writing

QUESTIONS

Once the basic forms of modern printed books for children are
known and tested on children in developing countries, how does
one write well for them, satisfying their needs for emotional
fulfilment, entertainment, information, sense of identity (personal, social and national) and any other needs that may have
been met by oral literature or older forms of printed literature?
Should the writer think of 'needs', or is it enough that material
be well written, regardless of audience? Are the literary styles
and forms used by writers for children different from those of
writers for the adult, general audience? Is the work of the
writer for children respected, or is it looked down upon as
inferior to adults' literature? Is there or can there be special
training for the writer of children's books?

HISTORICAL PERSPECTIVE

Many societies are passing from oral-based into print-based
forms of education. While there is a general tendency among
educators to deplore the disappearance of the oral materials,
there is at the same time a lack of understanding about the
process of transferring literature from oral to written or
recorded form. In many societies, oral literature for children
had, or still has, a highly prized entertainment value in addition
to the moral or social values it was intended to convey. When
transposed to materials corresponding to a formal system of
schooling, the entertainment value was often considered

'improper' or 'unsuitable' and was invariably left out. Hence, the same story with a moral might be told orally in a family compound and provoke laughter, music and dancing, but when put in a school reader, elements that would elicit this reaction were generally omitted, since such a response was not considered acceptable in the rigid order insisted upon in many school classrooms.

This 'cleaning up' or 'making proper' was common in virtually all European languages in the early years of children's literature. Most educators deplored the quality of the inexpensive chapbooks and picture sheets (meant for general mass consumption) that children were reading. Many of these chapbooks and sheets used story material coming from oral traditions; others simply dramatized and put into story form the unusual happenings of the day. By the time such material reached the format of books suitable for use in educating children, it was inevitably rewritten into sterile, didactic prose of poetry of little interest to children.

Consequently, two types of book publishing for children developed separately: (a) literature aimed at use during the child's free time, and (b) literature intended for school or formal educational use. The same versions of literature were rarely published in both types of book, although that did come about later.

Literature specifically written for the entertainment of children, and not based on oral sources, may have begun in Great Britain with the publications of John Newbery (1713–1767). The French critic Paul Hazard felt that this was a preeminent position the 'northern' or Anglo-Saxon countries maintained right on through the first third of the twentieth century, at least in terms of quality. There were several attempts from the seventeenth century through the nineteenth to produce children's literature in several European languages, but Newbery's early successes (both commercial and in terms of child appeal) were not repeated until the late nineteenth century, with only a few random exceptions. In the intervening years, children were forced to read excessively didactic tales, or to cull from adult or popular, street literature the stories they liked, or to listen to stories told to them.

Only a few critics have theorized to any great extent on the specific qualities of children's literature as distinct from literature in general. Authors themselves have differed widely on the subject, some stating that they most definitely wrote with children in mind and others that they wrote with no particular level in mind; their results were deemed literature for children by the editor of a publishing house, or by the audience that spontaneously developed for what they wrote.

Hazard included in the term children's literature both that specifically written for children and that written for a general or adult audience, but which had been taken over by child readers because of the peculiar appeal of the story. Another French critic, Isabelle Jan, is much stricter and includes in the term only books written for children. She excludes folk and fairy tales, on the grounds that they were as much for adults as for children. Even picture books are excluded, since she considers them a separate art form, apart from literature, owing to the importance of the illustrations.

Curiously, in the English language criticism abounds about distinct types of children's literature, and about specific authors. A great deal has also been written about how and when literature can best be introduced to children and what qualities it should have in order to answer different needs; but there is very little in the way of criticism of children's literature as part of the mainstream of all literature. Rarely is a survey of children's literature included in general histories of English literature.

In the USSR, Maxim Gorky became the champion of a special literature for children of the revolution. Above all, he stressed that it must not appeal to children through a lowering of literary standards, but through consummate craftsmanship. He pleaded for the inclusion of subjects about other peoples and races, so that a spirit of internationalism could be inspired in children. Gorky's influence has since pervaded the children's literature of all the Slavic-language countries.

Educators, rather than literary critics, have had a leading influence in some countries. Rousseau wrote that it was better to give no books to children, since authors couldn't seem to write without preaching or moralizing to them. Many educators misinterpreted Rousseau's 'back to nature' dictum and a flood of children's books pretending to teach natural subjects under an entertaining guise was the result. This was especially true in Germanic-language areas. Consequently, children's literature in German remained didactic well into the twentieth century. Illustrated books, however, did not. Those by Meggendorfer, and the picture sheets in the *Münchener Bilderbogen* series and others created a new type of popular literature for children that was highly entertaining and at the same time beautiful in its design and detail.

An educator, Lu Hsün (1881–1936), was the first to develop a modern theory of children's literature in Chinese. While Lu Hsün believed strongly in the importance of the old folk literature, he found much of it no longer valid or meaningful for children. He felt that a judicious selection of folk literature, complemented by modern Chinese literature for children, together with translations of some of the classics for children from around the world, was the best combination for present-day children.

During the past decade, a dramatic change has taken place in the literature for children published in the English-speaking countries, in many western European countries, in the Nordic countries, and in Japan. This has been the trend to include in children's literature the themes of modern social realism, heretofore thought inappropriate for children.

Folk and fairy tales contain many similar themes, but they are set in a remote past, and it was generally argued that children did not tie in these themes, except in an allegorical way, with their own lives. Psychologists, rather than literary critics or educators, have been the most interested in the effects of folk and fairy-tale literature on children, starting with Charlotte Bühler in 1918 and continuing down to Bruno Bettelheim most recently.

The trend of modern children's literature to treat in a realistic, present-day setting such themes as alcoholism, child abuse or abandonment, drug addiction, divorce, homosexuality, and racial prejudice, to name just a few, began in Sweden and the United States. There are still many parents and persons working with children who do not find most of such books acceptable as children's literature. On the whole, though, their acceptance is increasing.

This preoccupation with the problems of modern industrialized and materially wealthy societies means that many of the present-day children's books from the developed countries do not provide meaningful models for the developing world. They are simply too far removed from the realities of day-to-day living as experienced by children in the more traditional societies. On the other hand, some of the modern books deal sensitively with issues that need to be faced in all societies of the world, as for example concern for the environment. By showing writers and illustrators in other countries that even complex subjects can be handled well and be of interest to children, the development of good children's literature can advance rapidly.

PRESENT-DAY OUTLOOK

Do you have good writers for children in your country? How does one write well for children, satisfying their needs for identity, emotional release or fulfilment, entertainment, information, etc.?

Abu Nasr, Lebanon: There are some books in some of the Arab countries that are not suitable for children at all, I think. For example, in some, the content relating to the position of women is totally distorted, as it is also in some English books. I think some one should start questioning the image of women in Western books.

In Lebanon, we are doing a study on the concept of woman in textbooks now. The old traditional stories are fine. However, do we want to perpetuate or to accept the fact that a woman should be submissive, that a woman is a slave, and that a woman should be married at the age of 14 and that it is God's blessing to have many children? Are these really the values we want to impart to our children? They were once our traditions. But time changes traditions. Another thing that we lack in our children's books is poetry. A great deal of poetry is written, and our children recite a lot of poetry in school, but those words are so big and so meaningless for most of them.

In Lebanon and Egypt several writers are trying to write for children. We have Rose Rayev in Lebanon. Her style is simple and beautiful and easy to read for children. Mrs Rayev writes for children in colloquial Arabic. This is still something that is not accepted, and yet if you write in classical Arabic children do not understand what you are writing. So no one wants to write for children.

Jafa, India: The general quality of writing is still not of a high order. There is a lack of child-oriented stories having a childhood appeal. There is also a general lack of originality and good presentation, the style of writing and themes selected by the writers are quite often didactic or too adult in treatment. The entertainment aspect is also commonly overlooked. This is not to say that there is no quality writing at all. In fact some titles are very well written both in form and content, and some writers are endeavouring to write something original and worthwhile.

Most of the publishing for children is oriented towards meeting the requirements of the schools, either for textbooks or for supplementary reading. In the field of creative writing, most of the work in recent years has been concentrated on the rewriting of folktales, stories from the Panchatantra and Jataka and other classical and mythological stories.

Creative writing in the English language is a recent development, but in Hindi and some other regional languages this has existed for a long time. Thus biographies, heroic and other stories, and nursery rhymes have been written. However, there is very little for the pre-school and the beginning reader. Full-length fiction for juveniles is also scarce.

Kudat, Turkey: In my view, the most important type of children's book needed in the Turkish market comprises books which offer the child the elements of abstract thinking, innovativeness, and fantasy formation. To offer these elements is particularly important in a country like Turkey, which incorporates people of different ethnic and cultural characteristics, so that the messages communicated do not have validity for just one group at the expense of others.

Raratabu, Fiji: In countries like ours in the Pacific, where we are mostly newly developing nations, it is important that we maintain our cultural and national identities. In order to participate in our nation-building, our children need to be educated so as to create in them a spirit of patriotism as well as love and concern for people in other countries. As of now, in countries like Fiji, children often have a higher opinion of white people than of other races, including their own indigenous race. Fiji, like other developing countries in the Pacific, needs publications that will educate its own children about important people who have contributed so much to the development of their country. It is important to publish, in the Fijian language, biographies and autobiographies of national heroes, statesmen, chiefs, Christians and others.

Segun, Nigeria: As there are very few writers for children in Nigeria and very few children's books produced in the country, one would say, rather, there is a lack of awareness of the importance of suitable literature for children. Because of the high percentage of illiteracy in the country, attention is focused more on textbooks than on non-textbooks for children, especially since the commencement of universal free primary education in 1976.

This lack of awareness on the part of educational authorities and others involved in the upbringing of children is apparent in the extreme reluctance of publishers to publish picture-books, story-books and non-fiction books for children, the tendency for booksellers to stock mostly school textbooks and readers, the paucity of school libraries, especially in rural areas, the absence of neighbourhood libraries to cater for children's book needs after school hours, the many homes without books for children. It is also significant that, until very recently, when a Children's Literature Association of Nigeria, was formed by a group of volunteers, there was no special organization for the promotion of children's literature. There are no awards for writers and illustrators of children's books.

The effect of this lack of awareness is that writers for children find difficulty in getting their manuscripts published except where the books can be adopted as school supplementary readers. This has discouraged many would-be writers for children, and hence very few children's books are produced in the country.

As I stated in a paper written for the sixteenth Congress of the International Board on Books for Young People (IBBY) in Würzburg, Federal Republic of Germany (October 1978), 'There is need for creative, well-conceived realistic stories dealing with modern universal problems such as broken homes, alcoholism, drug abuse, teen-age problems, parent-child conflict; and local problems such as child-marriage, polygamy, the extended family, superstition and fetishism . . .'

Oral literature (folk-tales, rhymes, riddles, etc.) and literature that concerns modern life are equally important. Oral literature is a part of a child's cultural heritage that helps to give him a feeling of cultural identity and a sense of pride in his ancestry.

However, too much looking back can lead to negative thinking, which would not help a developing country like Nigeria to progress in this technological age. This is why I deplore a situation in which there are hundreds of folk-tale books while only a handful of books depict modern life.

In a developing country, life is changing fast, and children are encountering problems never faced by their parents. The generation gap is made wider by the new Western culture superimposed on traditional culture. Children stand between these two cultures and are confused. Realistic stories woven round these problems would help such children to sort themselves out. As the saying goes, 'Self-knowledge is the beginning of wisdom.' Reading about other children in plights similar to theirs would help them to examine their own emotions and find ways of solving their problems.

Made to measure: children's books in developing countries

Uribe, Venezuela: To write well for all children in a developing country means selecting from oral, traditional materials and editing them carefully; it means selecting modern themes from the real world of children, and developing them in language of quality that does not talk down to the child. It is not a question of proportion between the two types, with one being more important, but rather that they each express their truths in convincing ways.

Traditional materials help children in getting to know and appreciate their own culture. This is important in developing countries, where there is a tendency to underestimate what is ours and to consider good anything that comes from developed nations. Also, and this is very important, old stories and legends are rich in knowledge of human nature, wise in the problems humans encounter when learning to live together. In most cases, their message is one that is still alive today and one that children easily grasp.

Modern materials related to current themes, close to what the child sees and hears every day, are indispensable for promoting reading, and also for helping children to recognize themselves, their surroundings and their circumstances. It is a unique emotional experience for children—and for anyone in a country that imports most of its books, films and television programmes—to realize that children like themselves or their friends can be the characters of a story that happens in a street like the one nearby. That is, that the world and people surrounding them, and not always strange and faraway people and lands, can be described in written language and published, for all to read.

Modern materials are much more difficult to obtain, at least in our experience, compared with the easily available and very good traditional stories. Many authors who have already published have a very traditional, didactic and moralizing approach. Curiously enough, this is also common in many young authors who have not yet published. On the other hand, a few of them reject traditional approaches, insisting on innovations, but too often limiting these to formal aspects—for instance, abandoning the conventional horizontal text—without really contributing to a greater communication with the child reader.

Ediciones Ekaré avoided dealing with authors in the first books they published by selecting stories from an Indian tribe and adapting them themselves. In this way we hoped to show prospective authors the simplicity, directness and humour we wanted in the texts for the very young readers. It is too soon to appreciate whether or not we have succeeded in conveying our objective, but a few interesting manuscripts have arrived since then and we are working on one of them with the author.

Is the children's writer treated with respect?

Mirhadi, Iran: There was once a lack of respect for the writers for children in Iran, but this is no longer true. The social, educational, psychological and also economic attitude towards childhood has changed and continues to change. From being considered only a stage of maturation it is now accepted to be an independent stage of growth with its own characteristics and needs and thus its own writers, illustrators, publishers and institutions.

The promotion of general education and the insistence of more than 8 million young readers in Iran has made writing for children a social and economic challenge.

It is true that many Iranian writers for children write also for adults, taking up occasionally general social or political problems and ideas, presenting them in fairy-tale and legend form, but some authentic, talented and capable Iranian authors and poets have stepped forward. They have devoted most of their works to the young generation. They are loved and respected, accepted and criticized according to their works.

Two very significative decades of continuous work in the promotion of children's literature—seminars, national and international meetings, lectures, technical articles and books, establishment of children's and school libraries, interviews and mass-media work, book lists and prizes—have helped authors and illustrators of children's books to receive an increasing attention from the public.

A young generation of authors brought up in the joy and love of reading is also making its appearance in Iran.

Segun, Nigeria: One might be tempted to think that writers for children had won some recognition in the country because a veteran writer of school primers and readers in a Nigerian language (Yoruba) was awarded an honorary doctorate degree by the University of Ife a couple of years ago, but this was more in recognition of his contribution to formal education than as a writer for children.

Villaluz, Philippines: No. There is no lack of respect. 'Lack of interest' would be more accurate. The children do not select a writer because he is popular. They do not follow a 'fan-like' interest in a particular writer. It is the story they are interested in and not the writer. Yet, there are instances when the author is like a Pied Piper to his readers. But this author stops writing. Why? It is probably because the publisher cheated him/her on royalties. In this manner, I can say that some publishers 'lack' respect for the writer. In particular cases, however, when a writer submits a series of children's stories to a magazine, for example, then he develops a following. He also gains the respect of his readers and other writers. As a matter of fact, this method is used by many publishers before they launch a certain author's book.

Is there or can there be special training (formal or informal) for the writer of children's books?

Raratabu, Fiji: Lotu Pasifika Productions does not write materials for publishing. We sometimes organize writers' workshops where teachers and others can learn the art of writing. In most cases the written materials are offered back for LPP to publish. Some secondary and tertiary institutions have their own writers' training classes, but in most cases their articles are published in school magazines that are produced yearly.

Jafa, India: Children's Book Trust, a publishing house devoted exclusively to providing good reading material for children, has recognized the dearth of good writers. The Trust has organized a Writers' Workshop to train and guide aspirant writers of children's books. The Workshop is free, and the work of several participants has been published by the Trust itself. The Workshop has evoked a very good response. To encourage good writing, the Trust has also started an annual talent search competition. The response to this is also very encouraging.

Illustration

QUESTIONS

Once some of the basic forms of modern printed books for
children are known and tested on children in developing
countries, how does one illustrate well for them, satisfying their
needs for visual story, entertainment, information, sense of
identity, emotional response, and any other needs that may
have been met by visual experiences in earlier times? Are there
different levels of 'visual reading' development in children,
depending on cultural training as well as environment, or is
such development a purely physical characteristic that prog-
resses automatically and universally in much the same manner
as other physical growth?

HISTORICAL PERSPECTIVE

There have been visually 'readable' materials produced by
and for humans for at least 50,000 years, but we have no evidence that any of the prehistoric or early historic art was
specifically by or for children. After the invention of writing,
but before printing, we do have some illustrated documents
and manuscripts produced specifically for children. These
were usually for children of ruling families, or for those
meant to learn some religious beliefs or duties through
stories and pictures. Examples of the latter are the Chinese
pien-hsiang. These were pictures of incidents illustrating
narrative events in Buddhist scriptures. The invention of block
printing, and later of movable-type printing, simply spread

the availability of these materials to a wider group of children.

One of the first illustrated books known to have been designed for children and to have actually been used by large numbers of them in all European countries was the *Orbis Pictus* of Comenius, which first appeared in 1657 or 1658. There were probably close equivalents in Chinese or Japanese printing, but the evidence to show widespread distribution of a single illustrated text among children in China or Japan has not been uncovered.

The *Orbis Pictus* was followed by only sporadic examples of illustrated print material specifically designed for children. Rather, European and North American youngsters continued to enjoy the picture sheets, woodblock prints, chapbooks and other illustrated items being produced for the adult general audience, and distributed in ever-greater quantities. One has only to look at the fascinating plates in Sigfried Taubert's magnificent *Bibliopola, Pictures and Texts about the Book Trade*, to note that children are frequently included among both the buyers and the onlookers at bookstalls, at the packs and pockets of itinerant sellers, at fairs, etc. It was only in the early nineteenth century, however, that children's literature as such began to appear on a regular basis in the West. In Asian countries (outside of China and Japan), children did not see as much printed visual material, but the sequential narratives drawn on temple walls, the shadow puppet plays, the picture cloths of itinerant story-tellers and many other devices served to introduce illustration to a broad segment of the child population.

The exceptions to this were children growing up in Africa and Latin America and in areas influenced by orthodox Islam. The latter had materials available to them with decorative, but little, illustrative art. The former groups, including almost all American Indian groups, had little for children that was visual in their cultures in a narrative sense. Although the importation of books and magazines, and the later development of television in some areas, has changed completely the visual experiences of some young children in developing countries, others remain relatively untouched by visual narrative.

Therefore, the introduction of picture story-books and other visual reading materials will probably have a different impact on different children, depending on what the history of illustrative material has been in their area. Some studies have attempted to determine visual understanding and preferences in print media among peoples not widely exposed to such media. There have also been studies on colour preferences among children and adults, when observed in print formats.

These studies provide valuable information for the illustrator working with children's materials. They need to be supplemented, however, with further studies on the understanding and preferences of children when shown illustrative material of a narrative quality that can be identified with oral narratives commonly known to all in a given society. For example, the data in *Communicating with Pictures* (Nepal) are extremely helpful for the illustrator creating a series of alphabet charts or cards, or one doing posters or wall sheets. In these cases, individual pictures and the ideas conveyed by them are of paramount importance. But to convey modern narrative 'story' illustrators will need to know more about how traditional narratives that already exist in visual form are perceived by children. In Nepal, for example, this would mean putting some of the temple friezes that relate to Buddhist birth stories into printed form, and testing to see whether children make the same visual 'reading' of the printed form as they do of the temple frieze form.

In other places, locally familiar folk-tales depicting stock characters and situations would have to be illustrated and then tested. Research among rural children of Iran has shown that, although very few had an opportunity to see a wide sample of illustrative art, virtually all recognized illustrations that were stock representations of historic and folk characters, the 'devil', etc. When such children were asked to draw or paint one of these stock characters or creatures, even if they had not seen a printed visual representation, they seemed to depict them in a remarkably similar fashion.

Frequently, in books dealing with the Western child's responses to printed illustrations, one will find statements to the effect that children will accept, and even prefer, a wide variety of illustration styles, a wide range of colours and designs. More recent research is showing, however, that while children (especially young children) will tolerate looking at a wide variety of illustrative styles, if an adult is looking with them, their responses are vastly different from adult responses, and if observed objectively and carefully, they seem to narrow their preferences when the choice is theirs.

There is still far too little research, even in countries with an extensive picture literature for children, to be able to say definitely that there are some universal responses in all children to colour or line in printed form. The little research that does exist seems to point to the fact that young children having their first exposure to visual material in a print format seem to be able to understand the content best in illustrative material that uses flat, primary colours and firmly defined lines. However, this does not necessarily indicate aesthetic or artistic preference.

Other research, including some among older children, seems to indicate a preference for the realistic rather than the abstract. But again, most of this research was done with the idea of narrative content as an important basis of illustration, and this automatically conveys a bias against the abstract. I have personally used the rather abstractly illustrated book by Leo Lionni, *Little Blue and Little Yellow*, Astor-Honor, New York, 1959, in many different countries and with many different age-groups and types of children. It is invariably liked and understood, on its own, provided one gives a few clues, especially to children with almost no experience in handling books. Often, the translation of the title alone is sufficient for the non-reading child to understand and appreciate the book, or to appear to enjoy it even without understanding the narrative. This leads me to believe that we cannot so easily dismiss abstract illustrations as being of little interest to children. In the hands of a gifted artist, and with a text as effective and simple as that in *Little Blue and Little Yellow*, abstract art can obviously be quite satisfying and universally appealing.

Pictorial narrative, an aspect that makes illustrated books easy to understand when exported to other countries, is also the aspect that is, in a sense, most dangerous. Dangerous because the tendency has been to declare these books 'universal' and to accept them in such numbers that they overwhelm any efforts at local production of similar materials. There are sufficient studies to prove that unless children see themselves reflected in at least some of the books that are considered to be the best in their cultural milieu, they will continue to have negative images of self. Earlier studies among black children in the United States were particularly revealing, showing an extremely low self-image. Sufficient evidence was there to indicate a direct correlation with the fact that they only rarely saw themselves depicted in the visible culture of their society, and then often in a degrading or stereotypic manner. Much has been done to rectify this, but there still remain, even in countries with the most highly developed materials for children, large pockets of minority-group children who never see positive images of themselves and their group reflected in the printed or electronically produced images that prevail in their society.

Developing countries need to choose carefully the imported materials used with children. It is, of course, important that children also see and come to know those who are different from themselves, because that, too, helps to define the self-image. But care must be taken that imported items, however beautiful, do not acquire so much status and prestige that they automatically seem 'better' than locally produced materials. Fortunately, many of the countries with advanced production of children's materials have published some items that artistically reflect the cultures of diverse groups in many parts of the world. Such items should be imported more than those that are good examples reflective of Western cultures.

Another form that has not been tried out sufficiently in developing countries is the 'toy' or 'trick' book that is indigenously designed and produced. The best examples of these have shown themselves to be powerfully attractive to children, and a strong inducement to reading. Since they require a great amount of hand labour, they have become too expensive to produce in technologically developed countries. Colombia has established itself as a production centre for such materials, but so far all the titles produced have originated with publishing giants from highly developed countries. More publishers in developing countries could experiment with simpler forms of 'trick' and 'toy' books of an attractive, well-designed nature, with local content. The labour-intensive aspect of such publishing is less of a deterrent in developing countries.

Finally, serious artists must face up to their social and artistic responsibilities to the young in their societies. There are artists in virtually every country, but few have made the effort to explore (without compromising their artistic integrity) the special needs of children *vis-à-vis* plastic and graphic arts. This does not necessarily mean that the art will reach the child in the form of illustrated picture story-books. There is also something to be said for sheets, posters and collections of art reproductions that show the best modern and historic art traditions of a country. These are expensive to reproduce, and should certainly not be the first books produced for children in a country. But some developing countries are already producing such materials for adults, and they could make careful selections and redesign the formats so that they would appeal to children. These materials could be used by national and local governments as special gifts and prizes for outstanding work or scholarship by children, by industries as special awards for attendance, production, etc., and by other groups or organizations. There are materials in each country that allow children to see their own artistic heritage in as favourable and aesthetic a presentation as the materials now being imported.

PRESENT-DAY OUTLOOK

Are there good illustrators in your area? Do serious graphic artists make good illustrations for children?

Hirsh, United States, with illustrating experience in India: As far as I have been able to observe, the situation is not very encouraging. Serious painters and graphic artists are basically interested in following their own artistic evolution, and with few exceptions (notably *Home*, illustrated by K. S. Kulkarni, Children's Book Trust, New Delhi, 1965) are not interested in the field of children's books. When a painter or graphic artist does attempt to illustrate a book, there is often a greater desire to follow artistic fashion (often imported) rather than to illustrate the content of the story. Commercial artists seem to resort to a cartoon or comic-strip approach that falls far short of the potential that good children's book illustration should offer. Traditional artists are often reduced to turning out copies of past art works or minor items for the handicraft boards, gift emporia, or tourist industry. To my knowledge no traditional artist has yet attempted a children's book. There is a great need for the recognition of illustration in general, and children's book illustration in particular, as a valid form of artistic expression. The Children's Book Trust has made serious attempts to further this recognition, with some success.

Shah, Kenya: There are very few young children's titles that are published locally. Most lack colour and pictures. It is difficult for a young child to be able to appreciate a book of an environment different from that which he has experienced. It is also important that children's books have colour and illustrations. However, if all the cost has to be borne by publishers, then the books would not be within reach of many, as print orders are likely to be very small. The only way would be some sort of subsidy from government or some such body. Once this sort of subsidy is available more titles could be published in a more acceptable way and marketed vigorously.

Uribe, Venezuela: There are many excellent artists in Venezuela. The problem is, for the moment, guessing which of them, young or experienced, 'serious' or humoristic, will understand the needs of children in relation to books. We have preferred young illustrators with little or no experience in books, and we have learned together (on the job) with results that we regard as satisfactory. Team-work has sometimes been difficult and time-consuming but has usually enabled us to achieve our main objectives both in the literary and graphic aspects.

We tried to work, on one occasion, with a relatively well-known painter, but he would not accept suggestions either from the editors or from the art director and finally decided not to produce the book and to go back to his painting, where he felt free, unfettered by the limitations imposed by text and the demands of a child audience.

As an illustrator, have you been given good texts to illustrate?

Asare, Ghana: I feel that some of the texts I have been given to illustrate were rather uninteresting even for adult readers, and some were not well edited. Some of the texts, I think, resulted from the authors' own excitement, which they did not have adequate skill to convey to young people, also editors have had too little experience with children to really know how to help create the wider scopes and newer worlds that books should set out to create, especially for young people.

I have also been given texts which I felt were not based on solid enough information where they needed to be. Some had been written and edited so unimaginatively that it only became possible to illustrate them after meetings between the author, editor and illustrator. In my own experience I have had to make corrections and suggestions to both authors and editors in order to have situations in the text in which my proposed illustrations could really complement the work.

This does not mean that I have not had really good and well-edited texts to illustrate. Considering the experience and technical skill available here, I must say that it is only the smallest number of texts that have not come up to the mark.

Calvi, Brazil: The books which I have illustrated in Brazil (eighteen in print and three in preparation) all had the texts and formats selected and finalized before I was given them to illustrate. There has never been an opportunity for author, editor and illustrator to integrate the work in a final product.

The texts are of a heterogeneous quality and at times have been rather mediocre, often owing to the fact that the books are selected and edited more for their political and social aspects than for the appeal or interest they have for children. There is now in Brazil the beginning of a greater consciousness of the importance of well-written children's literature that is also presented with quality graphics.

Can a good children's book editor provide useful guidance to the illustrator or do his/her comments serve more to restrain the illustrator?

Asare, Ghana: Guidance from a children's book editor can be useful but not important to a versatile and well-informed illustrator in order to produce the best illustrations. An editor may live in a world apart from an illustrator in terms of what it takes to make good illustrations.

An editor's sophistication must extend to the widest cultural realms in order for his/her criticism to be meaningful and constructive for the illustrator. Otherwise, the editor may even tend to restrain the illustrator's artistic adventure and creativity, which are often necessary instruments in illustrating.

However, a good illustrator can use the guidance of a good editor to determine appropriate characters and backgrounds as well as to maintain consistency and style. I find editors' criticisms useful when they draw my attention to such points.

Calvi, Brazil: This is not only important, it is fundamental. It seems to me that the true editor is one who succeeds in extracting from the author and illustrator the best text and images that can be achieved. Criticism is basic to one's work and stimulates the illustrator to do the utmost to enrich and complement the text. In countries like ours, which tend to utilize very little of the richness of inherited cultural identity, it seems to me that one of the functions of the editor is to stimulate and suggest ways in which the images can be more representative of the cultural and visual aspects of the country.

What experiences in the visual or cultural background of children would influence their acceptance of and interest in illustrated children's books?

Hirsh, United States, with illustrating experience in India: Most Indian children, rich or poor, still have access to a grandparent or other adult as a personal story-teller with time and patience to unfold the traditional myths and legends, filled with gods, demons, heroes, princesses, kings, queens and wise and clever animals that form one of the greatest repositories of story in world folklore. The colourful language of these stories requires a colourful exposition in the illustration of this traditional material, or even in contemporary material, in order to seem at all appropriate to the children. Most children I have met, as indeed most adults, seem almost unaware of the rich painting traditions of India. Still, the choice of colours in clothing, homes and temples (which often abound with highly polychromed dieties), not to mention the film posters and films themselves, show that intense colour is absolutely necessary to daily life and equally necessary, I would say, to children's books. There is great scope in adapting styles from the miniature and wall-painting traditions, which not only serve as fine models for illustration but also re-introduce the child to his or her cultural heritage. The contemporary illustrator, as long as he follows the action of the story clearly, in bold, colourful, forceful illustrations, will surely capture the child's interest, no matter if the style is traditional or modern.

How can the children's book illustrator best be trained?

Asare, Ghana: I have personally found a course in educational psychology and constant touch with children very useful to my work as illustrator and writer of children's books. I think I can communicate with them more effectively because of this contact with young people and wish the same for all artists who want to illustrate for children.

I also believe that illustrators of children's books must be

Made to measure: children's books in developing countries

very extensively educated so that they will have lots of information or know where to get it. They must really be able to produce illustrations that do not merely complete the books but also extend the scope as well, even set trends for young people.

Exposure to a wide variety of children's books that have proven to be effective as well as travel and exchanges is very necessary in developing first-class illustrators in the developing countries. So far, what we have achieved has been out of raw talent and very little else.

I find good illustrations of children's books very stimulating and consider it very important that one be exposed to illustrated children's books from all over the world. The kind of books that have been most inspiring to me are those that were not just written, edited and illustrated with some pictures, but those that were planned, written, edited, designed and illustrated so that the pictures and the text were artistically integrated on the pages. Such books are indeed works of art in every sense and have made use of the best techniques in designing and production. The pictures are not complicated or out of fantasy. Their tones are not wild and gaudy but well controlled, even delicious. Usually, they look very simple and easy and so timeless and clean.

I have my favourites in line drawings, such as the pictures in René Guillot's *Paulo and the Lioness*, Margery Gill's illustrations of *Paulo and the Wolf*, etc. I also have favourites in the form of other monochromes that are not drawings but prints and other creative uses of ink and textures. One example I have is the book entitled *Thistle and Thyme*. Of colour illustrations, Japanese artists have particularly impressed me with their simplicity and good colour sense. I also enjoy Russian children's books except that I do not like their cheap form (mostly limp backs). From the West, which provides the largest number of great illustrators and books, I admire artists like Vera Croxford, Felix Hoffmann, Robert Lee, Charles Keeping, and a score of others.

Calvi, Brazil: It seems to me it is fundamentally necessary [as an illustrator] to see and to experience the work of other artists. I believe that the exchange of experiences with others stimulates in each one work that shows the artist's particular search for the appropriate graphic expression. Some illustrators I have known personally, such as Maurice Sendak and Tomi Ungerer, are living examples of the dedication, discipline and spontaneity that show in the work they produce. They inspire in me a desire for professionalism and authentic expression that stem from the unleashing of their talent.

The technical aspects of reproduction and printing, of colour separation, etc., seem to me to be basic to the formation of the illustrator. Artists, who in general have very little of this technical formation, need it as a minimum in order to design or create while thinking ahead to the final, printed product. It is important to fix in the mind of the illustrator the idea that the printed book, and not the original picture, is the final artistic product. To understand the concepts of page layouts and integration of text with pictures is also important.

I am not too sure if I agree that it is important for the illustrator to have an understanding of child psychology and the phases of child development. This is more a task that falls to the editor. It is more important that authors and illustrators do not lose their natural 'feeling' for children and what satisfies them. It can be helpful if the illustrator sees children's books that have been successful, and if someone who works with children explains the principal reasons for this success. I believe it is important even for developing countries to stimulate the criticism of children's literature, so as to help local authors and illustrators. However, I have not found that they do so in a manner and language appropriate for the stimulation of local talent.

The existing courses in art and design suffer from a lack of qualitative infrastructure (equally from professors and museums). In our countries spontaneous talents exist that are in general very rich and expressive. We should make it possible to preserve this spontaneity (and not lose it) so that our potential is enriched and we are oriented more towards a children's literature consistent with the realities of our country in terms of both language and images.

Editing

QUESTIONS

What is the role of the editor in selecting from the mass of older, existing material that can be reprinted or translated for children? What part should the editor play in stimulating, selecting and editing the work of new writers in developing countries?

HISTORICAL PERSPECTIVE

Editing children's literature as a profession is relatively recent, and even non-existent in a number of countries that produce children's books. Some sources cite Horace E. Scudder of Boston as the first children's editor in the English language. He was a contemporary and friend of Hans Christian Andersen, and edited for children's magazines as well as for book publishers. Most of his work was done in a manner that would be called 'freelance' today, i.e. he was not hired to be a full-time editor for all the children's materials of a given publisher, but edited individual books, series or magazines on contract.

The first full-time editor exclusively in charge of the total production of all children's materials of a specific publisher is generally conceded to have been Louise Seaman (later Mrs Bechtel), who was promoted to that newly created post by Macmillan in New York in 1919. Most of the other publishing houses in the United States followed suit in the 1920s. These new editors had generally been trained in education or in children's library work, and they usually came to their jobs with a fair amount of direct experience in using books with children although there were some notable exceptions.

From this time on, the tasks of the children's book editor have included selecting from the manuscripts already submitted those that should be published, working with the author on polishing and perfecting the text, soliciting additional manuscripts for other types of book deemed necessary to round out the list, selecting the illustrators to match each text (if the author is not also the illustrator), searching for texts to go with the work of a particular artist deemed worthy of trial, working with the art department to select the type, format and other design elements, working with the designer and printer on correcting proofs, writing (with the sales department) the copy for catalogues and advertisements, following the reviews in all the journals and newspapers, discussing with librarians and other institutional buyers the responses children have shown to the books, visiting bookstores to see what else was on the market, and keeping up with general trends in child development and education. All these were and are expected of the children's book editor.

Prior to the 1920s there were many persons doing at least some of these tasks in publishing houses in many parts of the world, but they were invariably the same persons who were also doing the job in relation to the adult books published by the firm. There was no perception of the need for different skills for children's materials. In Europe, this attitude continued in some countries until after the Second World War. Indeed, there are still quite a number of general publishers who have no specially trained editor assigned to the task of evaluating and editing their children's materials and seeing them through the illustrating, designing and printing processes.

Nowhere is the skill of the children's editor more needed than in the selection of those portions of oral literature that translate well to printed versions. Folklorists have rightfully decried the tampering with folk-tales, the watering down that has happened in so many cases when oral folklore was transcribed and then put into children's book form. On the other hand, the same folklorists are much too 'purist' when they insist that oral literature should not be changed at all when put into written versions. The successful editor is one who can select from oral literature those stories or segments that appeal most to children, and that need to have the fewest changes made.

Yet virtually all such literature needs some changing, if only to bring to the written version the same vitality that was present when the live narrator could indicate feeling with gesture, voice, musical accompaniment and a host of other devices. In this sense, the folk-tales collected and adapted by Jacob and Wilhelm Grimm are a success with children, even though they are not the 'pure' texts demanded by folklorists. It is up to editors to refine this skill, or to locate writers who are able to do so. Otherwise, modern children will turn away from their traditional literature in print form, because it has lost the freshness and spontaneity of live, oral narration.

In countries where oral tradition is still strong, narrators and story-tellers who are recognized among their peers as being the best should be observed and recorded (on tape and on film, if it can be done unobtrusively) as they recount to children. Teachers and others in the community with the gift of observing children should record the oral folklore of the children themselves. Editors and writers should be given the opportunity to study these recorded materials at some cultural centre where they may be stored, with the express purpose of determining what elements make the performance most appealing.

In effect, transferring oral materials and editing them require just as much work as writing new materials, in order to be completely successful. In all too many countries, such folklore (in versions for children) has been put down haphazardly, carelessly and with little regard for the requirements of written forms of literature. The recording of it by folklorists using established techniques and stringent accuracy is one requirement. The selection and minor adaptation, so as to put it in print for children are totally different but equally important requirements.

The seeking, training and guidance of new writers for children, especially those who can write contemporary stories and information books and articles, are another major task of the children's editor. There is a great dearth of such materials in developing countries, especially at a level suitable for younger children. More study collections will need to be set up, for writers and editors to learn together how others in different countries have collaborated to produce good writing for children. More examples of study outlines are also needed, matching existing books and materials, and showing how sensitive editors guided writers in perfecting their work.

Editors need to be trained in the subtle ways and methods of recognizing future authors. They need to be given sufficient time and funds to enable them to go and visit schools, child-study centres, libraries and other places where they can observe persons who have a special rapport with children, who know how to talk to and with children (without talking down) and who have a keen sense of 'story' in their use of language, regardless of the subject.

In many developing countries, writers may have to serve as editors for each other. Writers for children should be willing to have their work submitted to the same rigorous criticism as that meted out to the best of adult literature. Most truly successful writers for children around the world have a kind of humility in front of their child audience and a respect for it that have not yet penetrated deeply the ranks of writers in many developing countries. Perhaps in editing the work of their peers, and in being edited by them, they can achieve the stature they surely deserve.

PRESENT-DAY OUTLOOK

Is editing children's books taken seriously in your country? Are there special persons designated as children's book editors in your publishing houses? How do they perceive their role in selecting from the older existing material that can be reprinted, from translations, from new writers, etc.?

Mirhadi, Iran: Only a few publishers have an editorial board and a special editor for children's books. The Institute for the Intellectual Development of Children and Young Adults, the

Made to measure: children's books in developing countries

Amir Kabir Publishing House, and the Radio and Television Publishing Organization (Soroosh) are the only ones. Other publishers do not see the necessity and cannot afford it for two reasons: (a) most books they publish are translations of unimportant, mediocre, easy books and sometimes comics and trash; (b) they accept very few original works by Iranian authors, and if they do so they publish them on cheap paper with cheap print.

The editors at the above-mentioned institutions are not always successful in the selection of manuscripts, in their work with the writer and illustrator, in the selection of a book format, and in the resolution of printing problems. Nevertheless they have achieved some very exquisite books.

Considering the bulk of original works by authors of children's books during the last two decades, we can say that the few editors working in this field, such as Lily Ayman, Cyrus Tahbaz, Mahdokht Dowlatabadi, Tradj Djahanshahi and others, have had a great influence in the development of children's literature in Iran.

In several cases editors have tried planning, publishing and helping authors by guiding and giving incentives, but their work in general has been more accidental (examination and selection of texts submitted) and less constructive.

An exception should be made for the Reading Material Preparation Centre, 'Peik Magazines', which has a more highly trained editorial board. The centre organizes courses for the education of new editors of children's books, and the Children's Book Council planned a workshop for editors during the International Year of the Child.

Kudat, Turkey: The answer to this question requires a distinction between pre-school books and those for older children. Such a distinction is much more critical in the case of Turkey than in many other countries. The pre-school books lack originality and are predominantly translations from other languages. The translation criteria are the cost of copyright, size and feasibility of printing in Turkey. The lower the cost, the fewer the number of pages and the poorer the quality of paper and colours required, the higher the chances of a commercial printer translating the book. No conscious and systematic effort is made to edit it to suit the needs of child development. Children's imagination and fantasy are partially served, but factors contributing to the development of logic, mathematical thinking, language, the semantic structuring of the word, relevant values and the norms of cultural behavioural styles, are all ignored.

The translation of books for older readers, though still dominated by the same non-adapted form as that for pre-school books, has led to the appearance of some information books as well as a number of encyclopaedias. Although the above-mentioned needs are still largely ignored, national writers include many culturally relevant values, norms and behavioural styles in books for older children.

Jafa, India: Until recently, children's book publishing was mainly confined to textbooks, and book publishing for general reading was only a side-line. Fortunately, this is changing, and separate departments for children's books have begun to be set up by the publishers. This has given a clear identity to editors of children's books. The Children's Book Trust has also had great influence in the field of publishing books for children.

Editing of children's books is done either in a general sense or is confined to copy-editing. Sufficient editing is often not done and one can find glaring mistakes in published books.

The emerging new writers are sincere, and if told specifically what is expected of them and in what way they can improve the text they are willing to accept suggestions. Unfortunately, there are no facilities for training or guiding writers. Editors are also generally unfamiliar with the requirements of a children's book. Consequently, the writers receive very few suggestions and little guidance from the editors. Quite often an editor rewrites a promising manuscript instead of asking the writer to work on it.

There are no facilities for training editors, with the result that there is little understanding of the basic requirements of the field, which handicaps the editors. Most publishers have no clear editorial policy, nor can they spell out the editorial requirements to the writers.

Competent editors are in great demand, and a little experience in the children's book field is at present a sure passport for a decent job.

Njoroge, Kenya: The East African Publishing House has had a children's editor, working either full time or on a free-lance basis. We do not have one specifically detailed for the job at present—but the current editors are able to draw on the experience accumulated over some years. Manuscripts are evaluated with due consultation with primary education panels at the Kenya Institute of Education. If need be, the editorial department can always seek advice on any promising manuscript from teachers. In any case we usually have on the editorial staff somebody who has been a teacher in secondary school and who has had some contact with children and teaching needs. No actual testing is done on children—except in the preparation of course books. However, to ensure that we are on the right track, word lists have been compiled in the past, in consultation with Kenya Institute of Education experts, for different vocabulary levels.

Segun, Nigeria: Most well-established publishers give sufficient thought and care to the editing of the children's texts submitted to them. Others are not so painstaking. Local branches of foreign publishing houses tend to be more careful and insist on many changes. This can delay the publication of a children's book by as much as four years, especially when the editor is in the home country of the foreign publishing company and a lot of communication goes through the overseas post.

Sometimes these changes are for the better, but at other times they are not, the foreign editor firmly believing that he is the expert while the local writer is convinced that he (or she) knows what is suitable for the children of his country. This conflict may eventually be resolved through compromise or end with the capitulation of the writer, since he does not have many avenues for getting books published.

WA WA BULAN

Wa wa bulan!
Wa bulan cherah puteh
Di-mana rumah To' Wan?
Di-sini rumah To' Teh!

Wa wa wa......
Itu bulan!

ADEK BERTATEH

Taa-tateh!
Tateh sa-tahun lagi
Pandai berjalan
Pandai berkata.

Taa-tateh!
Tateh sa-bulan lagi
Boleh jadi
Bujang perkasa!

Adek sayang [Beloved Little One], *irama kanak-kanak* [nursery rhymes], collected by Azah Aziz. Kuala Lumpur, Penerbitan Akaz, 1970. Paper covers. A good example of a nursery-rhyme book that can be used as a lap-book (adult reading to child) or as a nursery school-book (teacher reading to group of children) or as a supplementary reader by children who have just learned to read. The illustrations are colourful and full of local motifs. Type size is large and clear with plenty of leading. Page design could be improved somewhat; paper should have been slightly more opaque.

लेकिन अगर तुम मुस्करा कर उनका स्वागत करो, तो वह तुमसे दोस्ती कर लेंगे। फिर तुम्हें उनसे डर नहीं लगेगा।

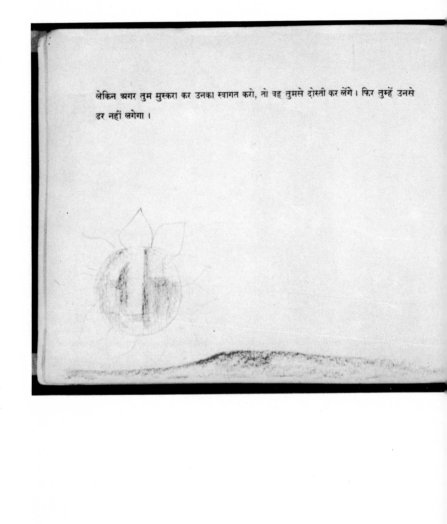

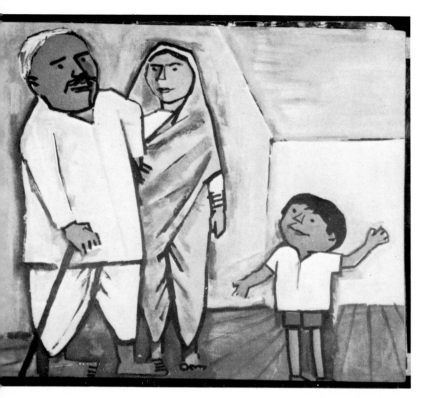

Ghar [Home], by Kamla Nair, illustrated by the author. New Delhi, Children's Book Trust, 1965. Paper covers. An outstanding example of a picture book that appeals to quite young children. The poetic, simple text contains the familiar and a bit of the different about home life. The use of the pencil sketches on the left-hand side of each double-page spread is surely an inducement for children to want to go off and draw their surroundings as they see them.

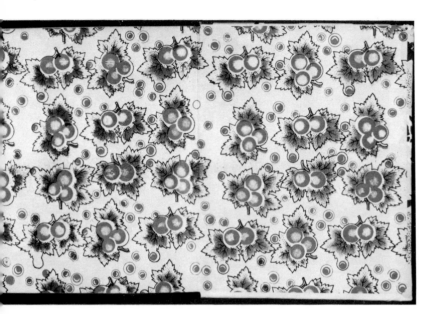

Madhumalati [Flower], edited by Al-Kamal Abdula Ohaba, illustrated by
A. Muktadira. Dacca, Ādita Adil Bros. and Co., 1964. 327 p. Board
covers. Cover and endpapers of a popular and attractive collection that
could serve as supplementary reading books in school or books to enjoy at
home. Selections include short stories, jokes, poems, short plays, biographical
and historical sketches, legends and even a few comic strips. Quality of
paper and reproduction of the illustrations are poor, but the books have so
much popular appeal that children probably do not notice these drawbacks.

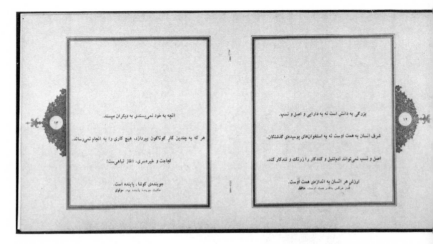

Farzand zaman naveshtar bash [Be Better, You People of the World], by Ghulam Reza Imami. Tehran, Institute for Intellectual Development of Children and Young People, 1972/73. Paper covers. An excellent example of book design adapted to a serious socio-religious subject for children. These are selections that give advice to young people, and form part of the literature that every Iranian child is expected to know, usually by heart. Note the use of decorative motifs only, rather than illustrations. Although didactic in purpose, the book is also a pleasurable, artistic experience.

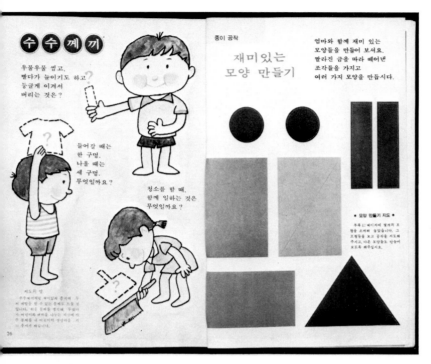

K'um-nara [Dreamland]. Children's magazine produced monthly in Seoul, Republic of Korea, by Yuk'yong chaedan [Educational Foundation]. A magazine for young children modelled on Japanese types, and designed for use in homes or educational institutions. Attractive and colourful in its production, it sometimes includes material suited only to much older children.

"Ovejita, La Motosa,
Tres días te estoy buscando,
Motosita, dónde estas?
Dónde estás, te has hecho daño?"

13

Después de pasar la lluvia [After the Rain Has Passed], by Carmenza Olaya
de Fonstad, illustrated by Patricia Durán. Bogotá, Clara Inés Olaya, 1977.
Board covers. A pleasant and old-fashioned look pervades this picture book
intended to introduce wild flowers and plants as a kind of subliminal
message beneath the story of a boy who loses and then finds his sheep.
Some of the double spreads are more attractive and effective than others.
Good quality paper was used, but binding and stitching are of very poor
quality, making the book fall apart after a few readings. This will prevent it
from having the wide use it should have in nursery schools, kindergartens
and early primary schools. The end-papers are a lovely evocation of a
rainshower.

CONOCE NUESTRAS AVES

42 AVES DE VENEZUELA PARA COLOREAR

BETSY TRENT THOMAS

Ediciones Ekaré-Banco del Libro   Fundación de Educación Ambiental

Conoce nuestras aves: 42 aves de Venezuela para colorear [Know Our Birds: 42 Birds of Venezuela for Colouring], by Betsy Trent Thomas, illustrated by Carlos E. Rodríguez. Caracas, Ediciones Ekaré-Banco del Libro in co-operation with Fundación de Educación Ambiental, 1978. Paper covers. A fine example of a mass-market book serving many needs, and yet considered fun by the children. While educators deplore the use of colouring books, children continue to find them satisfying. This one is redeemed by the fact that it suggests that the children go bird-watching in order to see the birds in their natural colours and habitats. In addition, it gives local and scientific names for the birds.

स्कूल में वे एक बड़ी नीली दरी
पर बैठते थे और छोटी छोटी
मेज़ों पर काम करते थे ।

एक दिन उनके स्कूल की
बहिन जी एक खुशखबरी
लेकर आयीं । वे बोलीं,
"आज हम एक नये दोस्त
से मिलने जा रहे हैं ।"

At the school they sat
on a big blue durrie,
and did their work at low tables.

One day their teacher
had a surprise for them.
"Today we are going
for a walk to see
a new friend," she said.

Shobhana, by Margaret Kidd, illustrated by Marilyn Hirsh. New Delhi, Children's Book Trust, 1968. Paper covers. Hindi and English versions of a pre-school picture book designed to help prepare the child for school and to teach lessons regarding traffic safety, co-operation, and respect for others. This has been used successfully in day-care centres, nursery schools, kindergartens and first grades. It is also appealing to non-Indian children at the same age level, as an introduction to some of the daily-life aspects of children in another part of the world.

Top: *Our Alphabet*, illustrated by Mara Onditi. Nairobi, Foundation Books, 1973. Paper covers. Bottom: *African ABC*, devised by Norah Senior. Pan African Books, in association with the *Daily Times*, Lagos, the *Daily Graphic*, Accra, and the *Daily Mail*, Freetown, 1959. Paper covers. These are the only two picture alphabets that could be located for Africa, and both are in English. The top one is also a counting book. The objects chosen for each letter are all from daily life and of interest to the child. This was designed as a supplementary text for first grade but is usable with younger and older children. The bottom one has catchier verses, and there is a bit more colour to the illustrations. This was meant for mass-market distribution and is a good example of three newspapers in three major cities of a region co-operating to produce an item having sales appeal for many of their readers. More co-production efforts of this type should be attempted.

So they rowed away, leaving him on the beach. Many canoes rowed away, but not one of them took him out to sea. "You are too young to go to sea," they all said.

Tawia Goes to Sea, story and pictures by Meshack Asare. Accra, Ghana Publishing Corporation, 1970. Heavy board covers with cloth spine. One of the few trade books of better quality issued in Africa, this was also published in a French-language edition. The text is remarkably free of pedantic or preachy elements; indeed the boy hero is rewarded for his artistic qualities when he might well have been scolded. The quality of paper, binding and price make this suited to institutions where it should stand up to repeated use.

atlamış atına... Dağı taşı alt üst edip kumru,
güvercin dememiş, girmiş kanına, Azrailin
kanına girer gibi... Bir de dönüp gelirken o
al donlu, al kanatlı melek atının gözüne gö-
rünmesin mi! Attır ürkmüş, kaldırıp yere vur-
muş, vurulasıcayı... Deli Dumrul bakmış ki,
ne baksın, Azrail tâ göğsünün üstünde değil
mi!

«Aman Azrail Baba, demiş; ben seni böy-
le bilmiyordum doğrusu. Başımdan büyük lâf
etmişim. Bir daha mı üstüne bir toz kondur-
mak, yedi ceddime tövbe olsun, aklım başım-
da değil; beni divane eden dağlar var, dağlar-
dan üstün bağlar var. O bağlarda üzümler
şarap olur akar; içtim içtim, duramadım; yi-
tirdim kendimi, bulamadım; demimi, devra-
nımı sürdüm ama, yiğitliğime doyamadım;
gel tatlı canıma kıyma benim!» diye aman
dileyince, Azrail:

«A budala, ne diye bana yalvarıyorsun,
ben de emir kuluyum. Yalvaracaksan, Allaha
yalvar!» deyince, Deli Dumrul yeniden delili-
ği üstüne almış:

Desene, bu canı bize veren de o, verdi-
ğini alan da o! Öyle ise, sen ne diye Allah ile

168

Dede Korkut Masallari [Grandfather Korkut's Tales], by Eflâtun Cem
Güney, illustrated by Neset Gunal. Istanbul, Doğan Kardeş Yayunlari,
1966. Cloth binding over boards. Illustration and textual page of a popular
retelling, for older children, of traditional tales. Although the illustrations
are rather poorly reproduced, the paper quality is good, as is general layout
and design. A generous amount of white space and a well chosen type-face
make for good readability. The cover is attractive and the binding is
superior. This company has produced a number of books of this type for
older children. However, they have not produced any books for the
pre-school age.

Cuando oscureció, el Rabipelado se subió
calladito al árbol y empezó a buscar al
Píapoco. Tocó arriba y abajo, aquí y allá,
pero por más que buscó y rebuscó
no lo encontró. Sólo se tropezó con
un paquete de ají tostado, cosa que nunca
le había gustado.

Por fin, cansado, se bajó del árbol diciendo:
— ¡Qué embustero, caramba, es mi
hermano el Píapoco!

El rabipelado burlado [The Opossum Who Was Tricked], from the
collection of Fray Cesáreo de Armellada adapted by Kurusa and Veronica
Uribe, illustrated by Vicky Sempere. Caracas, Ediciones Ekaré-Banco del
Libro, 1978. Board covers. An amusing folk-tale from the Pemón tribe,
living in the southern area of Venezuela, bordering Brazil and Guyana. This is
one of a series of indigenous folk-tales. A good example of an attempt
to bring the social and cultural heritage of a country to the attention of the
children, but in a manner appealing and interesting to them. This has a
wide age range in interest and readabi¹'ty. Sometimes the textual squares
are on the left and sometimes on the right.

● คนตรีบ้านป้าชาวตก่น หนุ่มก็ชักชวน
ค่างหัวว่าเริงสมใจ

● ชาเลิงกันคลอร้องเร้าไว้ เพลงจังหวะใหม่
ชา ชา แซมบาละตืน
● ถึงเทศกาลได้โดยอริล สมขารมณ์จิตน์
หนุมลขาช่าล่าละ

The music is exciting.   Whatever rhythm is played: Cha-Cha,
Samba, or Latin American, the youngsters dance fittingly.

Smosolwanolopburi [Lopburi Monkey Club] by M. L. Maniratana Bunnag,
illustrated by Ratana Atthakor, English text by Pharani Kirtiputra.
Bangkok, Kurusapa Pub. Co., 1967. Heavy board covers. An ingenious
picture story, inspired by William Pène du Bois' picture book *Bear Party*,
Viking, 1951. Both text and illustrations are completely new and fit very
well the Thai sense of humour. For younger children, only the Thai text
need be used, but the story and pictures are of interest to older children
who are often learning English as a second language. Since Lopburi is also
a tourist attraction, the book has sales appeal for tourists as well. The
design could have been improved by putting all notes at the end; footnotes
are out of place in a children's book.

Editors do give guidance in working on future ideas for children's books, but quite often such ideas are stillborn, as they are not followed up by the publisher. There is not that constant prodding of the writer that is a regular feature of publishing in more developed countries. A lazy writer, or a busy one, tends to shelve a project till a later date and then forget it completely.

Villaluz, Philippines: Most publishers economize on expense for editing. They are most likely to accept *per se* what authors submit to them. Some publishers pay editors on a per manuscript basis, selecting editors who accept the lowest fees, with consequent haphazard editing. When an author really wants to present smooth material, he selects his own honest and competent editor, who shares part of the minimal advance on his book royalty. Some publishers appraise the handsomeness of illustrations only, thinking that schools will buy the books based on the beauty of the illustrations. They consider that the illustrations, rather than the substance of the story, are of primary importance. This lamentable situation, I understand, is slowly disappearing. Nevertheless, such situations have existed for a long time.

How are manuscripts selected and/or solicited in your publishing house?

Njoroge, Kenya: After the East African Publishing House was set up in 1965 editors solicited manuscripts by visiting primary and secondary schools, and teacher-training colleges, and interesting teachers and students in writing. The early list of children's books has a large number of folk-tales, the writing of which was the initial response of EAPH's demand for children's literature. The first soliciting was a kind of general appeal, aimed at both discovering potential authors and obtaining children's literature. But there have been cases of well-known children's authors being approached for a particular kind of manuscript and being provided with assistance in conducting the necessary research: we have a number of titles (*Truphena*

Student Nurse and *Anna the Air Hostess* by Cynthia Hunter, for example), the writing of which was done with the help of EAPH-supported research. We have a series 'Our Nation' (for current affairs and civics books), made up of short books solicited from a well-known educator who has worked with the Kenya Institute of Education. In short, children's literature is solicited from people close to children's formal education. It is important to remember that in East Africa it is more realistic to think of school-going child readership than simple general child readership.

Raratabu, Fiji: We sometimes commission people who are already working with children, either in schools or in other educational institutions, to write about events, experience, etc., worth sharing. In most cases such people are not writers, let alone established authors, and therefore LPP helps where and when needed in the actual writing. Our problem is that few local persons feel committed.

There is an editorial committee that sometimes meets to decide upon the suitability of a certain manuscript by unknown authors, or about unsolicited manuscripts. The committee members are often expatriates. When local people are involved, quite often there is a lack of interest, enthusiasm and experience. Because of these problems the editing is often done without assistance from local sources.

The members of the editorial committee are people experienced in publishing, and some of them have behind them years of experience with children's literature. A market survey is taken on the need for a particular title. Personal contact is made with the Ministry of Education and other educational institutions for the publishing of complementary readers for schools and, on rare occasions, of textbooks. LPP has not, as yet, published a textbook for schools, but it is attempting and optimistically hoping to publish one or two titles to help boost its income in order to achieve economic viability. If the Fiji Ministry of Education considers our request sympathetically, we shall endeavour to take this approach in other countries in our region.

As we are the publishing arm of the Pacific Conference of Churches, we do occasionally work with our Christian Education Programme to obtain material prepared for use in Sunday Schools, for us to publish. More often than not the published books are translated and produced in local languages with only one being purchased from LPP.

Booksellers normally answer questions asked by LPP on the types of book children buy most in their shops. We invariably assess from these findings the titles we believe will serve the needs of our Pacific children.

Individual, interested writers sometimes visit our offices with unsolicited manuscripts, which on rare occasion brings to our notice some very worthwhile material.

What are the most difficult tasks of an editor in developing countries?

Uribe, Venezuela: As for the specific function of the editor, the most difficult tasks have been finding authors and illustrators, and then explaining to them the needs and interests of children in relation to books. Precisely because there is such scarce experience in children's books, it is not easy to find people with the necessary sensitivity and imagination to communicate with children, and who are ready to work on books for child readers. We have no doubt that many exist, but they are doubtless working in other fields. Once publishing for children becomes a serious proposition in Venezuela, many of these potential authors and illustrators will surely be recruited.

Design

Does the design of children's books and magazines differ greatly from that of materials for an adult or general audience? What are the respective roles of the publisher, editor and designer in creating books and other material that look and feel appealing, aesthetically satisfying and that fulfil the needs of children in their various stages of visual and motor development?

HISTORICAL PERSPECTIVE

Early materials for children, even those specifically intended to be used by and with them, did not pay too much attention to their special needs in terms of colour, visual clarity, readability and spatial sense. Only in physical size did the publishers seem to take children into account, but this may well have been because a smaller size was more economical and more appealing to the buyer (usually an adult), who found it 'cute' or 'charming'.

Many of the early books for children were beautiful and aesthetically satisfying, and children certainly appreciated them, especially if there was an adult introducing the materials. Nevertheless, many children probably kept away from printed materials because of their small or difficult-to-read type, illustrations that were often artistic but unappealing or confusing to children, or poorly placed as regards clarity and relationship to the text.

Even some of the beautiful materials produced for children in the nineteenth century, often cited as ideal, were not easily readable by children. This was mainly because few studies had been undertaken to determine the differences between adult and child visual acuity and perception.

There is a place for books with adult art and design standards in the life of the child. There is certainly a place also for artistic materials that cannot be read by the child, but are meant to be read aloud by a parent or other adult. But if one accepts that children need at least some furniture, clothing and environmental materials scaled to their needs, then one must also accept the fact that they need at least some print materials that they can manipulate, read (pictorially and textually) and appreciate on their own terms, without too much adult explanation and intervention.

This means that the design of children's books should be in the hands of persons who possess both a knowledge of the special physical and design perceptions of children and the talent to create good design. This is particularly important for materials destined for very young children, for those in the first years of reading experience, and for those with little or no exposure to reproduced visuals and designs in their culture. This means chiefly books with a large number of pictures, whether story or factual books.

Two early designers who chose children's book formats that were artistic and at the same time pleasing to children were Edmund Evans, a nineteenth-century printer in Great Britain, and Lothar Meggendorfer, an artist working at the same time in Germany. Evans is credited with being the first to design children's trade picture books as entire units, from cover to cover. He also introduced colour in pure, flat tones. There is no indication that Evans studied the particular needs of children—he simply liked beautiful books and felt children should have them as much as should adults. He instinctively seemed to select designs that appealed to children of that time.

Meggendorfer was responsible for bringing the design of 'toy' or 'trick' books (i.e. those with movable parts) to artistic heights not reached again until much later in the

United States. There had been many such books earlier, and they certainly appealed to children, if only because the movable part has always seemed to attract the child's attention. But they were generally of very cheap, poorly reproduced quality until translations of Meggendorfer's work began to appear on the European market.

Both types of book implied an adult reader or intervener. They were not intended to be read entirely by the child alone. In neither case does there appear to have been a conscious study of the child's response when alone with the books.

The first study that appears to have taken into account the child's response to design was Florence Eilau Bamberger's 'The Effect of the Physical Make-up of a Book upon Children's Selection', which appeared in the *Johns Hopkins University Studies in Education*, No. 4, 1922. Bamberger's research was much too limited to provide any real clues to the child's physical responses, as distinct from emotional responses. Since that time there have been numerous studies, but, as Barbara Bader points out in her book *American Picturebooks from Noah's Ark to the Beast Within*, many of them must be viewed with great scepticism, since they test 'the obvious by the available'.

Therefore, it would be pointless to summarize here the results of such studies, for there remains too much that is uncertain or questionable about the conclusions, especially as regards children in developing countries. More useful are the studies compiled by parents regarding the responses of their particular children to particular books. These can at least provide models for parents in developing countries who wish to attempt similar studies with their own children. A number of them are listed in the bibliography.

Publishers, editors, authors and illustrators in developing countries would do well to study the chapter 'Designed for Children' in Bader's book. It documents the attempts of a group of committed educators, artists, writers and publishers to produce the first books for young children (under age 5) that combined the interests of the child with the make-up of the book in interesting, artistic ways. This took place in the 1930s and 1940s in the United States. The end products were (and are) some of the finest books produced for young children in the English language, from the point of view of both the children and the adults reading them aloud. One can probably learn more about the design needs of a specific age-group of children by examining these books than from a wide range of studies.

This is not to say that objective group studies are not needed; nor will the results necessarily be the same in all countries, since children obviously come to reading with widely different backgrounds in visual experience. Suffice to say that design is an area almost totally overlooked by those producing books for children in developing countries; yet it is the design of the first print materials a child sees that may determine, more than any other factor, whether the child will look upon the act of reading as pleasure or consider it dull, uninteresting and undesirable.

PRESENT-DAY OUTLOOK

Do you feel that the design of children's books is important? Is colour a necessary factor in good design of children's books? Is there good design in your country's children's books?

Asare, Ghana: I strongly believe that the appearance of juvenile books is as important, and in certain cases more important, than their substantive content. This is especially the case of books for the very young. At that age they are more easily attracted by the purely visual. It is this appeal that arouses intellectual curiosity.

Looking beyond juvenile books, we must not ignore the strong cultural impact of pictures generally. Since culture is the image of a people's life, we must be right in thinking that the appearance of a book advances its flavour and tone more than words do. This is why in spite of films, television and novels of all kinds, picture magazines are still in circulation. The most effective and appealing illustrations have not always

Made to measure: children's books in developing countries

been in full colour. Creative use of monochromatic media, utilizing textures and good design sense, have achieved as much success as full-colour illustrations. Sometimes monochromes are even more pleasing because of their simplicity and neatness. There is a timelessness about them that is hard to attain with many colours. A look at the book *Heroes of the Bible* (Paul Hamlyn, London, 1967), illustrated by Robert J. Lee with both full colour and monochromatic washes, shows the strong stance of non-colour illustrations.

Calvi, Brazil: I believe that an aesthetically good book is one that is a pleasure to touch, to open, to see and to read. I believe that when all these aspects have been resolved, we will have an aesthetic of the total book. I find that a good book has text, illustration and design completely integrated.

The number of colours does not appear to me to be significant. More essential is the quality of the images and their appeal. To lower production costs, we should try to stimulate the use of one- and two-colour illustrations, but of the highest possible quality.

Jafa, India: Book designing is specially important in producing children's books, as it determines whether the book will make an instant visual impact and evoke the interest of the reader. Unless the book attracts attention right away, it is quite likely that it will not sell.

Cost of production of children's books is high, particularly when illustrations and colour are used. An imaginative book design can make a significant difference to successful publication.

Book designing suffers from lack of professionalism, and a vast majority of books does not possess the quality that determines young-reader appeal. Jacket design, binding, typography, use of white space on the page, placement and choice of illustrations and even the decision on where to begin a new chapter—in all these aspects book designing in India has a long way to go.

Who designs the children's books produced in your country? Is professional training available?

Asare, Ghana: I think professional art and design courses plus good general education count as the most-needed help of book illustrators in developing countries. Here, even where an illustrator has had some formal art training, he would not have been adequately exposed to techniques and media that will enable him to do superior illustrating.

Training in production skills, such as layout or format design and colour separation, could be useful, but in many cases we have production experts to take care of these aspects.

Jafa, India: Book designing as a separate discipline has not developed in India. One might even say that sufficient awareness of the need of a book designer as such is lacking. Also, there are no facilities for training book designers. This is not to say that well-designed books do not exist. In fact, some titles produced in recent years are very well designed.

The responsibility for book designing is shared between the editor, illustrator and printer. Jacket design is usually done by the illustrator.

Publishing

QUESTIONS

Who is publishing books for children: the state, private enterprise, public or private organizations, individuals, or a combination of all of these? Why do writers/illustrators of children's books act as their own editors/publishers in some countries? What are the chief difficulties in establishing publishing houses for children's books in developing countries?

HISTORICAL PERSPECTIVE

Virtually all publishing for children prior to the twentieth century was carried out by private individuals, organizations or companies. As mentioned before, publishers frequently combined the functions of editor/printer/distributor. A few specialized in materials for children, but most published adult and general materials, and added a few titles for children almost as an afterthought.

Some of the important early publishers for children were: John Newbery, Great Britain (eighteenth century); Isaiah Thomas and later Isaiah Thomas, Jr., United States (eighteenth century); Samuel Wood, United States (eighteenth century into nineteenth); School Book Society, Calcutta, India (1817–?); Dean and Son, Great Britain (nineteenth century); J. F. Schreiber, Germany (nineteenth century) ; Editorial Calleja, Spain (late nineteenth century) ; Hakobunkan, Japan (very late nineteenth century into twentieth) ; Harper (later Harper & Row), United States (nineteenth century and twentieth); McLoughlin Bros., United States (nineteenth- and early twentieth-century mass market); and Ticknor & Fields (later Houghton Mifflin), Boston, United States (nineteenth century and twentieth).

Religious organizations were also active publishers of material for children. It comprised mainly simplified versions of scriptural texts, or stories based on scriptures, or selections of scriptures that were believed to be important or appropriate for children. They were published either in local vernaculars or in the language of the colonial powers.

In Latin America, perhaps more than in any other area, publishing for children was invariably carried out by the author, who contracted with a printer for a fixed number of copies, and then distributed them in an often haphazard way, by gift or sales. Subsidiaries of Spanish publishers were often established in the Latin American countries, but prior to the twentieth century only rarely published materials by local writers. A few Argentinian publishers were exceptions to this rule, as were some periodical and newspaper publishers. The situation has improved somewhat in the twentieth century, but there is still much vanity publishing of materials that only rarely interest the child.

In the twentieth century some countries established state publishing houses for children's materials. The most notable examples are those in China, the USSR, Bulgaria, Czechoslovakia, the German Democratic Republic, Hungary, Poland, Romania and Yugoslavia. Publishers in these countries are expected to publish and distribute in large enough quantities to keep the price per volume very low. Much of the cost is recovered in sales through bookshops, but some subsidy is frequently necessary. Almost all publishing for children in these countries is carried out by a state agency or company.

Mexico and Brazil had very short-lived attempts at state publishing of non-textbook material for children of a very high quality in the 1920s and 1940s, respectively. However, the tendency in Latin America has been to have both textbook and non-textbook materials published by private, commercial firms, with the contents being approved by the appropriate government agency. Some exceptions are the Mexican text-books and the regionally published texts of the Central American nations.

Western Europe has tended almost entirely towards commercial publishers for texts, supplementary school material, and so-called 'trade' children's books. The state subsidizes only indirectly in a variety of ways. In some of these countries, public funds in fairly large amounts are used to buy books for schools and libraries, usually from approved lists. In others, booksellers are given rebates on books purchased outright by children, but again from approved lists. There are some trade publishers, notably in Italy, who must make economic ends meet entirely on sales through bookstores, because sales to schools and libraries are minimal. Most Asian countries generally have state publishing houses for textbooks and other school-related items, but the publication of trade books remains in private, commercial hands. There is almost no state subsidy of the latter, not even indirectly, because almost no public funds are used to purchase this kind of material in quantity for schools and libraries, except in Singapore and Iran. China has only state publishing and Japan has almost no state publishing for children, but does have some indirect subsidy through school and library purchases.

African publishing (south of the Sahara) was for many years dominated entirely by subsidiaries of British and French firms. In recent years, Ghana, Kenya, Nigeria and Zambia have made some effort to publish both text and trade materials for children using only local writers, illustrators and printers. In some cases, such publishing has been subsidized by government, in others not. In other African countries, even textbook publishing is at a minimal level or in the beginning stages. There is so little completely indigenous trade-book publishing for children that it averages out to fewer than one new title per year per country.

In North Africa and the Middle East, where Arabic is generally the language of instruction, the only country with a significant production of children's materials is Egypt. Sporadic commercial attempts to produce high-quality materials have been made in Lebanon but most of these efforts have come to a standstill. Tunisia and the Syrian Arab Republic both have state-supported units producing children's books in modest quantities. Textbooks, when they exist, are generally state-published in countries in this area.

While many consider the chief difficulty in establishing good publishing houses for children to be economic, there is much evidence to indicate that (in quite a few countries) a greater obstacle is the lack of understanding of the needs of present-day children in terms of printed and visual literature. This weakness extends to the creators, publishers, parents and other adults who introduce reading to children. It seems to take many years to develop a literature that is sufficiently diverse in format, design and content to allow all children the opportunity of finding something appealing to their tastes, interests and reading capacities. It takes even longer to convince parents and other adults that books are a necessity for children.

Whether the publishers are state, private or publicly owned corporations does not seem to matter, for there are examples of all types producing good literature for children. There does appear to be the need for publishers to operate less on the profit motive when producing children's books than when producing adult or general materials. This is especially true in publishing materials with limited market potential, such as books for gifted or handicapped children. Although necessary and useful, these publications rarely recuperate the amount invested in them and often have to be subsidized.

International co-publishing efforts have been successful in cutting costs in a few areas. Some publishers in North America, Europe and Japan have consistently worked out agreements on full-colour picture books, so that the plates can be printed in large enough quantities to make them economically viable. The texts are then added later in the various languages needed, or the black plate is changed at certain stages in the total run, so that the languages are printed during the same press run, one after the other.

Made to measure: children's books in developing countries

Another frequently used method is to sell only the photo separations to a publisher in another country, who then does an entirely local press run, using a translated (and often totally changed) text. This method is used very much by the mass-market publishers, especially for picture books and items licensed under internationally recognized agreements.

The co-publishing programme that has had the greatest impact on children's book production in a given region has been the Asian Copublication Programme, carried out for the past seven years under the aegis of the Asian Cultural Centre for Unesco in Tokyo. This project has produced eight volumes for children, each in up to fifteen different languages, but with national editions published in the participating countries. As Amadio Arbboleda has pointed out in his article in *Asian Book Development* (Vol. 10, July 1978), there has been some criticism of the project, in spite of its obvious successes. Among the criticisms he noted were: the lack of real experts on children's books participating on the part of many countries; sample editions that were too advanced in quality of production to have much meaning for many of the national publishers; no real proof that children liked the books; and poor selection of translators. I would add to this the fact that no titles were included for the pre-school and early primary age. This is the age-group for which virtually nothing exists in many of the countries, and the Asian Copublication Programme might take that factor into account. Nevertheless, it is an example of the ability of governments and private publishers to work together to produce children's books, even under very trying cir-cumstances. A great deal may be learned from the project, and programmes could be launched in other areas, so that the costs of colour separation, design, editing and the like are incurred only once, even though actual publishing takes place in a number of countries.[1]

1. Similar programmes are being launched in co-operation with Unesco through the regional centres for book development in Latin America and the Caribbean (CERLAL, Bogotá) and Africa South-of-the-Sahara (CREPLA, Yaoundé).—Ed.

Publishing

PRESENT-DAY OUTLOOK

It is generally agreed that a lack of good writers and illustrators prevents publishers from producing more good books for children in economically developing countries. What other major difficulties are encountered in publishing children's books in such areas?

Njoroge, Kenya: Obviously, financial restraint is the major problem, lack of enough resources and, therefore, some under-playing of the importance of children's literature, have a bearing on the availability of children's authors. Writers, by failing to enter fully into this area, do not develop their abilities in it. Our feeling at EAPH is that the country has a lot of untapped potential in children's writers; with enough encouragement and support, this second problem would be solved within a few years.

It is rather unfortunate that many publishers tend to give too much weight to producing for the lucrative textbook market at the expense of essentially creative children's literature. A locally based publisher with well-defined national educational goals would no doubt love to produce much well-illustrated general children's literature, but he continually feels the restraint of limited resources as he struggles to offer credible competition to the better-endowed overseas-based multi-national publishers. Obviously better availability of financing would enable more adventurous forays into children's literature publishing.

Raratabu, Fiji: The major problem is lack of funds to subsidize some of the publishing costs, so as to put the price of books within the reach of local people. In Fiji there are three major languages: English, Fijian and Hindi. There are already many English books, both from overseas and local sources, and Hindi books published in India. It is the Fijian language that is suffering. The Fijian Dictionary Project, which is not financed by our Fiji Government or even by the Fijian Affairs Board, lacks funds to continue its work. The Fijian language project of the Curriculum Development Unit of the Education

Made to measure: children's books in developing countries

Ministry faces a similar situation. My publishing company does not have funds for this. Our Fijian children are fast losing their language, and if nothing is done now, one major part of their identity will be lost.

Shah, Kenya: Half of the children's publications coming from overseas should not be allowed in. The situation now is that worthwhile books are not published locally because they are becoming really expensive to produce and market. Publishers and booksellers combined will not be able to compete with mass-produced books from other countries. They will need extra help from government by way of subsidy. Lots of self-restraint from booksellers, lots of sacrifices from publishers, and moral and financial support from the government would be needed to overcome the overseas competition.

Uribe, Venezuela: In our particular experience, the greatest difficulty is to raise funds for an activity that until now has not been considered relevant in the country. Fortunately, after many years of systematically pointing out the importance of children's books in the promotion of reading, Banco del Libro has been successful in this aspect, and both official and private institutions have given their support to its publishing programme.

Until recently children's literature was considered a secondary activity by both the author and the publisher. Only occasional publications were supported by different institutions dealing with children or education. With the exception of textbooks and supplementary reading meant to be used along with textbooks, no systematic and permanent publishing programmes for children existed until Banco del Libro launched its publishing department, Ediciones Ekaré, at the beginning of 1978.

What responsibilities do publishers have to children in general? Is the responsibility greater with regard to children's books than with regard to adult books?

Mirhadi, Iran: The young generation of today's world in Iran as well as in other countries, developing or not, needs everything: the past of its peoples, the wisdom of the old times and the experience of present problems.

If the importance of oral sources has been stressed, it is because the 'Western' style of living, with its standardized technical and cultural products, when distributed widely throughout developing countries, together with the great influence of profit-seeking mass media programmes, seems to bury with great speed the treasury of creative original works of art, literature and music, especially those from oral sources. There is a danger of uprooting the young generation and destroying its links with the past of its own people.

Much work has been done in this respect in Iran; many adaptations for children and young people have appeared during the last three decades. There is tremendous work to be done still, but what is lacking at present are books about the present-day children of Iran, their life experiences, their families in villages and towns, their problems and aspirations, and how they relate or do not relate these to the past.

In my opinion, much more work has still to be carried out. Books published lately show new efforts in this direction.

Uribe, Venezuela: We consider that a national publishing venture ought to give priority to national literature, especially in view of the particular problems which we have indicated. At the same time we are not suggesting an exclusive preoccupation with national literature. A selection of the best foreign material should be incorporated in any publishing programme from its inception, although in a lesser proportion than national materials.

While helping children to know and understand their own culture through national books, we should give them an opportunity to broaden their horizons by getting to know how children in other countries live, act and feel. Translated books may offer this opportunity if well selected and, obvious but necessary, well translated.

Made to measure: children's books in developing countries

What kinds of book do you publish for children? What kind should be published?

Njoroge, Kenya: Approximate numbers of titles produced in each category during the course of EAPH's work are: picture books for pre-school-age children, none; picture books for children in first years of school, none; modern fiction stories for children, age 8–11, twenty in English (about half of these are now in Kiswahili translation); modern fiction stories for children, age 12–15, sixty; folk-tales for children, twenty; rhymes, riddles and other oral folklore for children, none; non-fiction and informational books, twenty-five.

Which are the most important types of book for children in Kenya? This question is best answered by remembering that Kenya is a society still laying the foundations of formal education and literacy. Good textbooks, locally based and oriented, are a basic requirement in formal education. Kenya, indeed East Africa, requires far more elementary textbooks than have yet been published, and it is the aim of the East African Publishing House to contribute much more than has been possible to that basic area. However, local educationists have noticed a serious problem that cannot easily be solved with textbooks: a reversion to illiteracy for children who do not acquire more than primary school education. This problem arises from a failure to inculcate a burning interest in reading in the early years. Imaginative literature, produced in a graded manner in so far as language levels are concerned (in English or in Kiswahili) is therefore essential for shoring up both the formal educational aspect of the child's development and his cultural development. Aligned to imaginative literature, obviously, is factual informational literature, written informally and simply. The 'Our Nation' series, featuring civics education, is so written that the upper primary school child will learn while enjoying himself and acquiring the habit of reading. Our Primary Science Readers likewise offer exciting reading for young literates.

Raratabu, Fiji: Picture books for pre-school-age children, one; picture books for children in first year of school, one; modern fiction stories for children age 8–11, four; modern fiction stories for children age 12–15, five; folk-tales for children, one; rhymes, riddles and other oral folklore for children, two; non-fiction and informational books, six.

Do you get individual reports or feedback from your child readers?

Raratabu, Fiji: A brief and straightforward answer to this question would be no! Although we do not get regular feedback we do from time to time get encouraging and constructive comments, mainly from people interested in literature development. Occasionally we receive feedback from angry readers who express their frustration and disappointment because the published book does not mention anything about his/her island, nor has the picture any of his/her country people. As a result, they refuse to buy such publications. Some Pacific Island governments have strict control on books. Questionnaires sent to readers for feedback often get no response. This means that personal questioning gets the best reaction.

Distribution

QUESTIONS

Once a children's book or series of books is published, how is it distributed? Which distribution systems work in developing countries, where markets are either non-existent, hard to reach, or economically able to pay only a part of the cost of production per book?

HISTORICAL PERSPECTIVE

For a delightful view of some of the methods and styles of bookselling prior to 1900, one can turn to the plates in Sigfred Taubert's book *Bibliopola*, mentioned earlier. These iconographic representations show quite clearly that in Europe, North America, China and Japan there were booksellers of all types who carried materials of interest to children, even though they may not have been published specifically for them. In the twentieth-century trade, children's books have been distributed through the same channels used by publishers for adult and general materials, but with some additional variations. In the United Kingdom, United States and Canada, the usual present-day pattern is to have the great majority of books go to a few large jobbers, or distribution agents. These jobbers in turn sell to bookstores, schools, libraries and other institutions, but not to individuals. Some large bookstores and library systems purchase directly from the publishers, without going through the jobbers.

Mass-market books (including comic books) are usually

handled by separate jobbers, but in some cases a chain of variety stores or supermarkets will contract directly with a mass-market publisher for a regular flow of children's books in fixed formats to be sold in each of their store outlets. There are some books, such as paperbacks, distributed in mass quantities through school book clubs, that fall between regular trade and mass-media books. These books are generally reprints of proven favourites that have already appeared in hard-cover editions, but some are totally new. The individual teachers collect the money from children who wish to buy from a selection of about thirty titles each month at prices ranging from 40 to 75 cents. The teacher turns in the collected monies, together with the orders, and the books are then mailed directly to the classroom.

Textbooks are in many cases purchased directly by the schools from the publishers, and hardly ever go through jobbers. It is rare to find them for sale to individuals through bookstores.

Magazines for children are sold by subscription directly to the home, on news-stands, to individual children but with delivery via the school classroom, or to schools and libraries for classroom or recreational use.

The trade children's books in hardback have a very high percentage (ranging from 65 to 90 per cent) of sales to public schools and libraries. The trade paperbacks for children now coming into popularity have a lower percentage (than hardbacks) sold to schools and libraries, but it is still a significant amount. Therefore, with the exception of the school book club sales mentioned above, modest bookstore sales and family book club sales, the majority of books in these countries are purchased by adult professionals who work in some field of public service to children.

The publishers thus can target their promotional materials to a very specific group. Furthermore, a wide array of reviewing periodicals or journals with review segments describe and criticize a fairly extensive proportion of the new titles issued each month. Numerous selective lists are issued at regular intervals by institutions or organizations and these too are used as purchasing guides. A few large institutions maintain their own internal reviewing and selection systems, often writing critical reviews for up to 90 per cent of the total production of any given year.

Some have criticized this symbiotic relationship between the publishers and the buyers using public funds. Others have felt that too much power is wielded by a few key reviewers. Still others see it as a system that has served public interests relatively well, helping to contain costs and assure minimum sales on (and therefore a continuing supply of) all types of book, even those of interest to small, special groups of children.

This was not always the situation in the United States, Canada and the United Kingdom. Prior to the Second World War a very healthy percentage of trade books was sold through bookstores, department stores and toy stores. These were trade materials rather than mass market materials. True, quite a number were of the 'toy' or 'trick' book variety, but the text and illustrations were of a high quality; they were produced by the regular departments of children's trade book publishers, often at quite reasonable prices. There has just not been enough research to tell whether this decline in family purchase of children's books was from purely economic factors, or from socio-psychological factors (e.g. parents realizing they could get high-quality books free on a regular basis from their public library and therefore deciding they did not need to purchase them).

At the present time, relatively little promotion to buy children's books is aimed at parents, although this is changing in the United States and the United Kingdom. The difficulty is to assure availability of materials in bookstores, once they are promoted. If bookstores tend not to stock a wide variety of children's materials, and parents tend not to go to bookstores for gifts for children, it is hard to change these habits. Only some parents buy trade books regularly for their children, either in bookstores or through family book clubs.

In western Europe, children's book-buying patterns have been very different, with most buying taking place in bookstores. Because of rules protecting bookstores, even sales to libraries and public institutions must in many cases be made through a local bookstore. Until the last decade, only in the Nordic countries and the Netherlands have library sales been a significant proportion; but recent improvement and spread of library services to children in the Federal Republic of Germany and in France and Spain have raised the proportion of purchases from public funds. Austria, because of a nationally subsidized book club, is a case in itself. There the school is used as the main vehicle of publicity, but the children can buy their books at lower, subsidized prices at any bookshop.

The number of professional journals and organizations reviewing, listing or selecting children's books is also expanding in Europe, but it does not come anywhere near the total number doing so for English-language materials. However, periodicals and newspapers destined for the general reading public do have regular or occasional sections reviewing children's books.

Mass-market books are handled similarly to those in English-language markets, through special distributors. Textbook sales cannot be categorized for western Europe—there is too much variation from country to country and even from state to state within countries. But a high percentage are purchased with public funds. Magazines and periodicals are sold primarily by subscription directly to the home, or at news-stands. Outside of Austria, there are no children's magazine subscriptions or book club sales handled in mass quantities by the public schools, as in the United States and Canada.

In central and eastern Europe, distribution of all types of material is almost entirely carried out by the state, both for items used in schools, libraries and institutions and for those sold through bookstores and stalls, department stores, and the like. There is no differentiation made between 'trade' or 'mass-market' items; they are all 'mass-market' items because of the extensive quantities printed. Magazines and journals are sold at news-stands and kiosks, or through clubs such as the Pioneers, or through political youth groups.

Reviewing is done both by the professional groups, through journals or selected lists issued by methodology centres, and by literary journals and newspapers. Since the selection process of titles published for children in these countries is much more stringent than in Western Europe or the English-language countries, it is assumed that material inappropriate for children will not get published. Nevertheless, there is healthy disagreement at times as to whether a given item is appropriate, and some authors and illustrators are considered more talented and creative in their approach to printed materials for children.

China also distributes entirely through the state, but because libraries and reading rooms were so poorly developed, and because even the lowest sale price possible was often too much for some families to pay, a tremendous network of rental stalls grew up in the late 1950s. These were extremely popular with new literates and with children and youth, because they rented out mostly picture books that were extremely easy to read and had a visually appealing format. These stalls were closed for a time, but recently there has been a resurgence of them in many cities.

Finally, there is Japan, with its unique systems of distribution and a general public that probably buys more children's books per family than in any other country. Here, in addition to the usual sales through a network of special stores, stalls and bookstores, these are also large numbers of children's books purchased in sets from door-to-door salesmen, or via mail. There are countless schemes of this type, offering specially produced-to-order materials or items published by standard trade and mass market publishers. The sales to libraries, schools and other institutions are also considerable, although they by no means approach the percentages common to North America or some European countries.

With all of this different experience to study and reflect upon, how have developing countries approached the problem of children's book distribution? Have some tried to adapt the schemes used in technologically advanced countries? The answer to this last question is yes, but with widely differing results. First of all, in terms of mass market distribution, totally indigenous materials have enjoyed the least amount of penetration and success. This does not refer to materials translated and then published in a local language.

An early attempt at national mass marketing of children's books in a developing country was the 'Paisa Library' of Pakistan. Children who saved a paisa a day and sent their paisas at the end of the month to the publisher Darul Insha at Punjab would receive an attractive book of about a hundred pages. Because of economic difficulties, this scheme lasted only a few years.

Magazines were started by departments of education ministries in a few countries, with the intent of getting them into the hands of most children via the schools. In most cases this has not worked out—for several reasons: (a) the local school authorities have not undertaken to pay for bulk subscriptions for each classroom; (b) the magazines have to appeal to age ranges and reading levels that are too wide; and (c) individual classroom teachers are not trained in the use of supplementary material, particularly if it has recreational appeal as well, and fear that their authority will be undermined by such materials.

Consequently, many of these magazines have become defunct, or struggle along with minimal support and poor distribution. Exceptions are the magazines for new literates and children produced in Iran. Because these appeared for different age and interest levels, and used other means as well as schools as avenues of distribution, they have had a dramatic impact on the amount of reading material available to rural and small town children in Iran. It is said that the postal service improved dramatically in certain areas, because local people were so interested in reading the stories, jokes, poems, factual accounts and other diverse matter that they insisted on getting their weekly issues on time.

Iran is also one of the few developing countries that successfully adapted the public library system as a means of distributing materials for children and youth. Under the leadership of Lily Amir-Arjomand, the Institute for Intellectual Development of Children and Young People built and operated a system of some 300 libraries, reading centres and mobile units throughout Iran. Mrs Arjomand had received her training in children's librarianship in the United States, but the system she developed differed quite a bit from the North American type. It combined elements of the 'cultural palaces' for children common to the countries of Eastern Europe, and the 'Bal Bhavan' concept found in a few cities in India. Since Mrs Arjomand left the directorship of the institute in late 1978, it is not known what direction the work with children and books will take.

Another country that is experimenting with national library service to children and youth is Venezuela. The system is based on central libraries in each state, with eventual sub-libraries in each community and mobile units to cover rural and small town areas. All report to the national library, from which they receive partial support and services. Only the metropolitan area of Caracas is well developed, but a number of other states are well on their way to serving the main population centres. All experimental types of service, training, programming and the like are tried out first by the Banco del Libro, a private, non-profit-making institution that receives its funding from governmental and private sources. Experience in the system there has shown that the public library must be much more oriented to serving formal education needs than is common in North American patterns. It has also shown that it is extremely difficult to keep up the reading interest of children and youth, unless one has a continuing supply of materials that appeal to them. While the availability of Spanish-language materials for children is quite extensive, the greater proportion is simply not of interest to the modern young readers of Venezuela.

This has demonstrated once again the principle that library service to children and youth (whether public or school) is best attempted when a country has access to a minimum of 300 juvenile titles each year (combining locally produced and imported, but with emphasis on the former). With fewer titles, it is better for distribution using public funds to go out in small lots (or boxes), through day-care and nursery centres, health centres, school classrooms, community centres, factories, military posts and the like. Training in the use of this material with children should be offered to a wide variety of persons, and should concentrate on informal techniques with groups of children. One book used under such circumstances can usually serve several hundred children. The materials used should be those produced by commercial publishers as well as those of state publishers.

It may not be a good idea for most developing countries to offer direct state subsidy to existing commercial publishers. Most of the past experience has shown that this results in materials that are not the best for meeting the needs of children. Indirect subsidy seems to be a more effective means of assuring that a wider range of materials will be offered, from which those selecting for public purchase can choose on the basis of appeal to children, appropriateness of context, and quality of text, illustrations and design.

But it must be made crystal clear that unless government units put minimum requirements of such purchases into the operating regulations for each respective agency, it is not likely that indirect subsidy will ever work. Schools will have to be required to make annual minimum purchases of locally produced non-textbook materials for each classroom in order to pass inspection. Even the purchase of one book for each fifty children would have a dramatic impact. Similarly, day-care centres, nursery schools, kindergartens and the like, however they are operated or regulated, should have as a minimum requirement a certain number of pre-school books.

Other public and private agencies could also make an effort to build in a minimum but regular purchase of such material, to be used in an appropriate unit, either directly with children, or with parents who then use it with their children.

Only in this manner will public demand increase so that a constant supply can be assured in the local bookselling markets. It has been amply demonstrated in developing countries that parents (especially mothers) will spend a high proportion of whatever disposable income they have on their children. They must be given the chance to see the importance of recreational reading matter in the intellectual development of their children. Once this is clearly demonstrated in various public areas, distribution will be less of a stumbling block.

Made to measure: children's books in developing countries

PRESENT-DAY OUTLOOK

Is there a market for children's books in developing countries? If yes, is that market difficult to reach because of generally poor distribution systems?

Kudat, Turkey: The government, through the Ministry of Education, is the single source for the selection, development and distribution of textbooks. The private sector, on the other hand, monopolizes the non-textbook market, which is rather restricted on the demand side. The forces shaping the supply and demand structure for children's books are complex and have been explored in a paper I have written on the subject. In brief, they can be summarized as follows.

The Ottoman language evolved to meet the needs of the governing sector. Its formalistic concerns weighed heavier than its usefulness, which was restricted to bureaucratic purposes. These written materials were unintelligible to common people. The capacity of the Ottoman language to reach even educated children of the ruling class was minimal.

The educated ruling class was influenced by the European way of life. Child education mainly involved the acquisition of literacy and the learning of foreign languages so as to be able to read in those languages.

The rest of society kept its diversified character, with each ethnic group sticking to its respective native tongue and turning out indigenous literary materials only in an oral tradition. Religious education gave a small minority of the masses exposure to literacy, but without any pictorial description.

The tradition of authoritarianism in parent-child relations precluded the recognition of children's needs as separate from those of adults. Until recently, no need was felt to produce literary materials specifically for children. The few materials that have been produced tend to be either textbooks, with their rigid, content-specific standardization, or materials responsive to the needs and special requests of the upper strata of society, most particularly those in the cities and in the western parts of the country.

Njoroge, Kenya: This is not really an issue for us. Distribution in East Africa is easy. The problem is availability of children's books at accessible prices; when distribution through bookshops is not possible, it is always possible through schools, which are scattered all over the countries of East Africa. Of course, it is legitimate to argue that literacy is still being established on a mass scale and that books have not come to be as valued as they should be. But the current demand remains unmet owing to resource restraints.

Raratabu, Fiji: There are only very poor outlets for distribution throughout the country. Fiji consists of 300 scattered islands. Only the major town areas have bookshops. Rural folks occasionally visit towns, mainly to buy important domestic items. Co-operative stores are the only commercial outlets in those areas, so if these could be used to sell books this would help the less-privileged children. The road systems on even the main islands are still remote from much of the population.

Shah, Kenya: I believe there is a market for children's books. At this time we can reach the market in the following ways: (a) information sent or circularized through schools; (b) advertisements in children's magazines and other mass media (at present, advertising notices are taken as some form of higher truth rather than as advertisement); (c) bookfairs in smaller towns (these attract a lot of child viewers); (d) attracting children to bookshops by having some sort of competition (like colouring competitions and so on); (e) gifts to children in the form of books (book tokens can also be issued so the children may choose their own books); (f) publishers' and booksellers' combined efforts in publicizing the books by attractive display.

Uribe, Venezuela: The market for children's literature in Venezuela is generously supplied with literature from other countries. As a Spanish-speaking nation we import books from Mexico, Argentina and Spain, where many of the publications are translations from English, French, German or other originals. Because of the lower costs of these imported materials and the greater experience of the publishing houses involved, the main problem faced by any publishing initiative in Venezuela is not so much distribution as this type of competition.

Do you believe that books are still an appropriate medium through which to reach children? Have they been downgraded in importance because of radio and television?

Kudat, Turkey: Without elaborating at length on the theory of socialization, it should suffice to say that books have a definite advantage over other media, since there is neither governmental nor any other monopoly over their usage as an educational facility and since, they can be used by different agents of socialization—the family, teachers, peer groups, various organizations. Moreover, considering the costs associated with different media, books present yet another advantage. That no intermediary channels are necessary in bringing the books to children is also something to be remembered. They have a lasting effect, they can be used over and over if the child so wishes; their messages are less open to distorted interpretations; they can be distributed as gifts or loans and can be more easily made available as demand arises. None of this is true, for instance, of television or radio programmes, nor for the types of material used in formal public education.

Have you tried to promote the importance of children's reading and story-telling through mass-media types of wall chart and poster aimed at parents and teachers? Have you used such devices as book fairs to promote the sale of children's books?

Njoroge, Kenya: No, we have not yet published a simple wall poster or chart advertising the importance of reading aloud or telling stories to young children. Nor have we published a set of instructions for teachers and/or parents on how and when to use stories with children.

Raratabu, Fiji: No! We do not have sufficient funds for this purpose. There is a real need for this kind of publication because I believe it will help educate people on the importance of reading. Perhaps it would also help if wall posters to educate people to budget for their children's books were produced in a similar format.

Shah, Kenya: We have tried to have book fairs all over the country. This enables the general public to know what is available and so on. The fairs are held in open-air parks under tents, so many more people visit them than just usual book-shop-goers.

At such book fairs children's interest in books can be vividly seen by parents. Children's books should be displayed in such a position that adults see them when they are buying other items. We run newspaper advertisements during school holidays asking parents to buy extra reading books for their children's development.

Promotion

QUESTIONS

How are children's books used in the home, on radio and
television, in schools and libraries, and in other institutions?
How can this use be extended in developing countries?

HISTORICAL PERSPECTIVES

The original uses of almost all printed materials for children
were didactic, moralistic and expository.

Prior to the nineteenth century, few accounts exist of
how books were used with children, except for descriptions of
tutors or governesses and the manner in which they dictated or
read aloud from certain books. There are more accounts that
reminisce about the stories told orally than there are about
those that were read aloud. This seems to suggest that the oral
tales still had stronger appeal than the average printed story.

There are a number of early references to printed picture
stories. Goethe wrote the following in *Wilhelm Meister's
Theatralische Sendung* (Book 2, Chapter 5):

The folk will be most strongly moved above all by that which is
brought under their eyes. A daub of a painting or a childish woodcut
will pull the attention of the unenlightened person much more than
a detailed written description. And how many thousands are there
who perceive only the fairy tale elements in the most splendid picture.
The large pictures of the *bänkelsänger* impress themselves much
deeper on the memory than their songs—although these also captivate
the power of the imagination.

As mentioned before, all such picture sheets and chapbooks were a powerful attraction, making children want to learn to read, if only in a simple visual manner.

The nineteenth century witnessed a marked increase in the spread of children's literature in Europe and North America. Descriptions culled from autobiographies, journals or stories based on reminiscences of the period provide glimpses of how books were used in the home and in the school and the impact this had on children. (An extensive listing of such autobiographical writings can be found in Edith Cobb's *The Ecology of Imagination in Childhood*, Columbia University Press, 1977.) From these sketches we learn for the first time about the practice of reading aloud to children for entertainment as much as for instruction.

At the same time some churches began to offer free reading materials for loan to their members. Gradually, children's books came to be included in these 'Sunday School libraries', as they were called in Great Britain and North America.

Public libraries of the subscription type began including materials for children in the last two decades of the nineteenth century. Such libraries were common mainly in Great Britain and North America, and reached only children of families able to pay the annual fees. Free public library service to children did not start until just before the turn of the century, but it then spread rapidly throughout North America, Great Britain, the Nordic countries and a few other areas in Europe. For the first time, children of all social classes, even those from very low income families, could have access to a wide array of books and other reading materials. Furthermore, there were few constraints on the children's choice of reading matter. True, the mass-media types of book were generally not selected for public library purchase, but there was a sufficient variety among the trade books considered acceptable to give children at least some choice.

The real advantage of the non-formal approach of the public library lay in the fact that most reading there was not associated with assignments, homework or school requirements. Of course, there were instances in every child's life in which he

Made to measure: children's books in developing countries

or she was told by the teacher to go to the public library to get information on some subject, or to read a specific book for a book report. This is still true in areas where school libraries are not as complete or active as they should be. The public library children's co-ordinators, however, generally regarded their work in bringing children and books together as being quite distinct from formal school education.

Other agencies that began to include books and reading among their activities were the boys' clubs, scouting groups, and neighbourhood and settlement houses. These latter were (and are) social centres that usually served the low-income family groups in highly populous and crowded urban areas. They provided after-school recreation of many types, but were common only in North America. Clubs and scouting groups, however, sprang up in many parts of the world, and reading 'badges' and certificates were emphasized from early on; reading was also used to support interests in hobbies, collecting, handicrafts, outdoor life and other activities.

Teacher training began to include some acquaintance with the basic books of children's literature, and the weekly period of reading aloud from a recreational book acquired an established place in the curriculum, especially in the early primary grades. This is common throughout much of Europe, North America and other parts of the world with access to a wide variety of children's books. A modern device used by a number of school principals to stimulate reading is the weekly silent reading period when everyone in the school, from principal, to teachers, to students, to office staff, to cleaning personnel, must sit and read; they can read anything they wish, but they must read.

Home libraries started up, briefly in the United States and extensively in Japan, catering for a fixed group of children in a city neighbourhood. Some were publicly supported, but most carried on with private funds.

Family training books and courses also now include, in most cases, a segment on the importance of reading aloud to children, beginning with the very youngest on. There are still far too many people who do not take this seriously, but the greatly increased demand in the past few decades for books for the pre-school age is only one graphic demonstration of the fact that more parents do read aloud than did before. Freeburg and Payne, in a review of 'Parental Influence on Cognitive Development in Early Childhood' (*Child Development*, Vol. 38, 1967), cited some of the research evidence that points to an increase in intellectual curiosity among children who are read aloud to on a regular basis from a very early age.

Other places where children congregate or have to wait, such as doctors' surgeries, clinics, aeroplanes and other long-distance transport, hair-dressing establishments and the like, soon began to offer playthings and recreational reading material for children as a matter of course. Such items were usually magazines or mass-market productions, often not well selected, but they nevertheless reinforced the idea that reading was an enjoyable and accepted way to occupy one's time. Furthermore, children's books that helped to prepare children for a hospital stay or for some other painful event they had to endure became more and more prevalent. Reading took on still another facet: bibliotherapy.

Radio, films and television in North America, Europe and a few other areas utilized children's literature to a great extent, and thereby increased the demand among children to have the same material in print format. Case after case can be cited, in which the appearance of a story in a non-print form increased dramatically the demands of the child public to have the same story in book form.

These varied uses of children's literature have scarcely been attempted in developing countries. (Some of the exceptions have been noted in the previous chapter.) Although most discussions related to the needs of children focus equally on their physical, intellectual and emotional requirements, the fact remains that the international agencies, bilateral, multilateral and private, have channelled most of their assistance to meeting physical needs.

Where assistance has been directed to projects related to the intellectual development of children, it has generally been through formal school systems, even though there is much evidence that they are not meeting the needs of children in developing countries. This is understandable in that leaders of developing countries perceive the formal school system, with all its faults, as the only way of providing their people with the means to realize their intellectual and creative potential. Not enough has been done to demonstrate effective non-formal methods.

Another factor contributing to the slow pace of improvement in children's books and other materials is a scarcity of well-qualified experts who can deal with situations in developing countries and inspire innovative kinds of response in local personnel so that they quickly learn how best to adapt international experience to their own circumstances. This creates an environment in which children's books many sometimes be produced, but they are rarely suited to the real needs of the country and bring about little change and few observable results.

Governments will have to decide whether they wish to continue the disproportionate amount of attention paid to formal systems of education which can inhibit the development of locally produced children's books of the recreational type; there is a large body of evidence which indicates that formal school systems are extremely difficult to change from within, once they have adopted certain materials and techniques.

More mass-media techniques must be used to introduce the idea of children's literature and the importance of reading to children. Whether it be by radio, television, wall poster, or any other device, there must be much more intensive promotion to convince parents of the necessity of reading to younger children and providing older children with pleasure reading. Parents, especially those who cannot read, must be convinced that telling stories to their children is also important; even the parent who cannot recognize a single letter or word can usually point to a picture, say the word, and ask the young child to repeat it. They can be given picture stories to 'read' aloud to their children. Illiterate parents must be assured that they can prepare their children for learning to read almost as well as can the literate parent.

Persons being trained to deliver basic services to children

in rural and hard-to-reach areas must also have some training in how to introduce the concepts of reading preparation, story-telling and picture-reading to mothers and others who care for children. Virtually every traditional society will agree that oral stories are 'basic' to the child's education; the task is now to convince them that printed stories play a similar role in the life of the modern child.

Manufacturers of staple products that are purchased by even the lowest-income families should be encouraged to package such products, when feasible, with an attractive covering containing an illustration, which is appealing to children, and interesting readable labels. Some might even be persuaded, as a public service, to include a purely recreational reading text and some pictures not related to the product.

In short, a general consciousness of the importance of pleasure reading for children must first be aroused, by whatever methods seem best suited to the country. Following this, there must be steady public support, often indirect, for the few good nationally produced children's materials. The tasks of the specialists in the creation of better children's books are outlined in the next part.

How do you see children's books being used in the home in your country? Are there too few homes that can afford books? Or is there a large enough middle class and lower middle class that could be encouraged to read more with their children and buy more books for them?

Jafa, India: The availability of attractive books for just good reading is very limited. A 1973 survey shows that out of a total of 14,064 titles published, 387 were produced in India, placing it sixth in the world. Most of the books published are intended for school reading; that is, children's books written to order and not the self-expression of imaginative writers presenting their feelings in prose or poetry in such a manner that they can be enjoyed by a child reader. Most of the well-produced books are in English, yet this is the language only of the élite class or of those children who go to English-medium schools. The vast majority of children have, therefore, to depend on books published in the fourteen regional languages. Except for a few, the books published in regional languages are generally unattractive. Well-produced books are also expensive to buy. Besides, except in large cities, bookshops stock only textbooks, and it is not easy for parents or children to buy other books. The use of books in the home depends on whether the reading habit is encouraged among the children. This interest relies on the awareness of parents and teachers of the need to give books (other than textbooks) to children. Even in homes where the parents are conscious of the fact that children should be given books, they are often not aware of what a child should read. Thus, even in homes where the parents have money they tend to spend it on buying comics or other pleasures. Lack of easy access to bookshops and libraries makes the use of books even more difficult than it should be. Taking all the languages together, the number of homes where the reading habit is encouraged is quite large, enough to support an innovative publishing programme.

Kudat, Turkey: The answer to this question depends upon the segment of society one chooses to take as the target group. If the target is specified as the middle- and higher-income groups in the metropolitan areas, there will be no difficulties in introducing books to homes at reasonable prices. Institutions serving the urban rich (e.g. private schools) might also purchase such books, if they do not significantly cut their profits down. However, the urban poor and the rural population do not habitually buy books for their children.

A tradition of subordinating children's behaviour to the will of adults has prevailed, especially in the rural areas. With the household functioning as the production unit, the children's behaviour revolved around the activities of production, planned and controlled by the adults. The families were characterized by a high rate of fertility, and the large number of children taxed heavily the spare time of the parents, leaving very little for parental attention to the individual needs of each child. Culturally, the father was not expected to devote much time to the education of the children, particularly for the supportive interactions—including book reading—that are time-consuming. The mother, on the other hand, had neither the competence nor the time for such activities.

Do you see any future in public library development in your country? Do you think this can supplement the work of the schools or is it a needless, double expense?

Jafa, India: Public libraries have been developing in the country, though progress has been slow. Even the growth of school libraries has not been very rapid. The main reason for this is lack of adequate funds. As the cost of books is high and a vast majority of people have a low purchasing power, the development of public libraries is necessary to encourage the reading habit. This fact is recognized by the government and also by parents, teachers and book publishers.

Schools also put greater stress on textbooks than on just good reading. The school syllabuses are generally heavy and leave children little time for other creative pursuits. Education is also generally perceived as a means of securing employment and not so much for enriching the mind, with the result that the reading of general books is often not encouraged by parents or teachers.

Kudat, Turkey: A borrowing system designed through communal libraries might be one solution. Another solution would be to alter the habits of the upwardly mobile sectors of the urban poor and the rural population so that they come to want to purchase some books, provided that they are offered at very low prices.

Apart from still being incomplete, the public school programme has the following shortcomings: since it aims at standardized instruction, it makes up a rigid, content-specific demand for publications; there is no conception of auxiliary material to supplement the mainline curriculum; since a lot of red tape is involved in the public sector once a book is adopted for teaching purposes it becomes very hard to change what is taught in schools. This built-in inflexibility also brings with it the danger of teaching outdated information.

Uribe, Venezuela: Reading promotion and helping to establish permanent reading habits are basic for us. In Venezuela, 10 out of every 100 children never get to school, 36 out of 100 abandon it after the third grade, and some studies settle illiteracy around 37 per cent. These are facts that cannot be overlooked by any publishing programme in our country. Fortunately, our editorial work is linked to the establishment of a nation-wide public library system which we feell is indispensable not only for aiding formal studies but also, which is very important, for making books available to those who have had to abandon school. Public libraries are an alternative to formal schooling and an effective means of consolidating reading abilities in a developing country. Publishing programmes for children can play a fundamental role in achieving these goals by providing the necessary reading materials that respond to the child's interests, needs and reading ability.

PART III

Steps in the right direction

The following suggestions for improving the production and distribution of children's books in developing countries have been formulated within three broad categories: first, countries with virtually no production of any children's books; second, countries with national textbook industries; and third, countries with some annual production of most types of children's material.

In the least developed nations, with virtually no local production of any type of book for children, the following questions should be raised:

Is it better to start with textbook production or with production of books of the entertainment-information type or both? Some factors to consider would include: whether it is less expensive to continue purchasing mathematics, science and arts textbooks from abroad and to produce local textbooks in the areas of reading, writing and the social sciences; whether it is possible to produce books that are principally entertaining and informative and that can be sold through trade and mass-market outlets and at the same time serve as textbooks; whether non-book forms (e.g., picture sheets, charts, flyers, small magazines, etc.) should precede any book production, especially if there is already cultural acceptance of such forms.

For what ages and social groups should the first children's books be published? Some factors to consider are: Which groups can be reached most broadly and effectively? Which groups have been shown to respond the best in other developing and developed countries?

In what language or languages should the first books be printed? Should they be bilingual? Factors to consider include: Has there been careful testing of the needs of children in local language areas before such an important decision is made, or has the decision been motivated by political issues? What has been the experience of other countries in producing children's books in several languages? Has the expense been prohibitive? Have the results shown clearly the advantages of printing at least some materials in the home languages of the children?

Given the dearth of really good children's writers and illustrators in any country (developed or developing), and given the fact that all countries should be seeking to give their children broadened international outlooks, what should be the ratio of translated/imported works to total indigenous production? Some points to consider include: Should the country allow distribution of any and all types of children's material, regardless of their origin, as long as importers and distributors are willing to handle them? Does the economic power of large foreign commercial or government distribution agencies overwhelm local production efforts, and if so, how can this be countered, without impeding the free flow of information?

Such questions could be debated at national policy meetings involving a variety of persons from formal and non-formal education systems, social welfare units, ministries, and commercial printing and publishing firms, however modest, operating in the country. Such a group might well decide that the questions cannot be answered until further data and research are available, but the aim would be to get as many answers as possible, however tentative.

In developing countries where children's book production exists almost entirely in the form of textbooks, emphasis might be placed on attempting to determine whether the kinds and amounts of textbooks being produced are responsive to the country's needs. Additional factors to be examined should include:

Are the non-formal areas of education being served with the types of book now being produced?

Do the books available at present lend themselves to self-instruction or individual use without a teacher?

Should the allocation of funds be spread out to include production and/or purchase of other types of children's book, or children's literature in other forms?

In developing countries where children's book production exists in the form of textbooks, trade books and mass-market books, national policy meetings could be convened to examine the same questions as those mentioned above concerning the least developed nations, but from the point of view of past experience. Rarely is a national meeting held that discusses all types of children's book and other media, and the relative amounts that governments are spending on each type. Periodic re-evaluation is necessary to verify whether the spending is valid, whether more production money should be put into one type of book than in others, or even whether the money could be spent more wisely on non-print media. Public spending and private purchasing power need to be evaluated in context, one with the other. The use of materials in non-formal systems of education should be given as much attention as their use in formal education systems.

TESTING AND OBSERVING

In the least developed nations far too much children's book production (all types) has been based on copying and adapting models from more developed countries without any previous testing on local children, and observation of their reactions in a variety of situations. In some cases testing has taken place, but in an abstract or partial manner, or only under formal educational conditions in schools. This is particularly true of illustrative material taken out of context. For example, in many

Made to measure: children's books in developing countries

cases, representative groups of children have been shown a series of pictures, usually printed one to a sheet or card. Based on whichever answers the children give, the researchers will conclude that children do or do not understand, or do or do not prefer, certain types of illustration in books. In fact, the responses will generally be quite different depending on whether the children are shown the same illustrations during the narration of a story attached to them or during reading of a sequential series of informational points.

Many more projects need to be designed to test children's books that have been carefully selected and purchased from the production of other countries. As far as possible, these should include a variety of books with varying contents, but all related as closely as possible to the needs of local children. The texts should be translated by two or more translators and the translations hand- or machine-printed and skilfully pasted into the original books. The resulting books should be tried out on a wide variety of children under controlled conditions. Care must be taken to include trial in formal and non-formal educational settings, as well as in informal family situations, but always observed by someone capable of recording both parental and child responses. Abundantly illustrated books should even be tried out with non-literates or new literates.

When a sufficient number of books has been tried out in this way, it is possible to assemble the first data on the specific types of language style, illustration style, format, etc., that arouse the most positive responses in children. The results can be studied by those who are involved in children's book production, and will invariably be of help in inspiring improved local production. The most successful of the books can then be printed in an authorized local version, using the translation that was most enthusiastically received.

An excellent description of just such a project in Senegal can be found in *Wilson Library Bulletin,* October, 1979. Such programmes are not costly, but they must be given long-term commitment so as to insure continuity and viable results. Ideally, this type of programme would be autonomous and would serve as a focal point for information on children's books of all types, how they can be produced (even by hand), and how they can be used. Support could come from several ministries or departments.

In addition to the above programmes, small groups of authors and illustrators could be given the task of writing, illustrating and designing some of the basic prototypes of children's books that are needed in every society aiming at literacy. Examples include alphabet and number books, first reading books, folk-tales drawn from oral literature, and books providing information about basic scientific concepts in a clear and simple manner.

This could be done in training sessions held in conjunction with the programme outlined above, so that the prospective authors and illustrators would have the benefit of the ongoing research. The hand-made prototypes they would write, illustrate and design would also be tested with children, and the most successful could then eventually be commissioned in a final form appropriate for printing. Again, it must be stressed that these first books must be tried out in formal and non-formal educational situations, as well as in home use. It is of the utmost importance that these first books gain acceptance among the widest possible audience. They should not be as limited in use as are textbooks.

For countries that have decided that other forms are equally or more important than books, programmes similar to the above should be carried out using posters, wall charts, flyers, simple magazines, newspaper supplements and other printed material that stimulates reading. Again, the same system of trial and testing should be followed, using prototypes at first and printed versions later. There is much less experience here to draw on, since such devices were used in developed countries in previous centuries and their use today in developing countries is very limited.

Some that might be tried out include: picture-story sets modelled on the *kamishibai* of Japan, or the street-singer charts of sixteenth-to-nineteenth-century Europe; wall charts or posters that tell sequential stories in pictures, continued each week or month; one-page weekly newspaper supplements;

weekly or monthly flyers of one page, easy and cheap to place into or along with some object or service already being distributed reasonably well on a regional or national basis; inexpensive weekly or monthly magazines.

The motivation to read should come chiefly from the entertainment and pleasure value attached to the materials. Children are especially responsive to this form of motivation, whereas other reasons are too abstract and seem to have little bearing on their daily lives.

In those countries with some textbooks, but no other locally produced children's books, testing should be carried out to see how useful the textbooks are in non-formal and informal educational settings. Since it may take some time before all children attend school, some method must be found to make the locally produced educational materials useful and attractive to out-of-school children as well. Changes and improvements in existing textbooks should be made accordingly, especially if at the same time their usefulness in formal classrooms can also be enhanced.

Countries with some textbook, trade book and mass market book production should also test and observe the usefulness of each type in formal, non-formal and informal educational settings. If careful testing shows that one type of book is more effective in all situations than the other two types, a decision could be made to improve the quality and quantity and to distribute that type for use in many places. Educators might be given the opportunity and encouragement to try teaching of reading without formal textbooks.

Reading-interest surveys could be carried out, but not in the usual, general manner that groups books under such vague terms as 'adventure stories', 'animal books', etc. Rather, specific lists of all reading materials available to a given group of children, during a given time, should be noted. The frequency of use by the children can then be charted and the results should be defined within the framework of the total reading material available to them, cited by type and titles.

For example, if 100 urban schoolchildren and 100 village schoolchildren are given the same set of books, magazines, charts, picture sets, etc., and are then observed and questioned over a year's time on their use and enjoyment of these materials, it is not enough simply to list their use of these materials. Careful documentation of any other items the children have available in their homes, the abundance or dearth of visual and verbal advertising and other public signs in their environment, and all such related factors should be taken into account when determining what true reading 'interests' are. Final results and conclusions should state specific preferences by titles, as, for example:

The single title read and asked for most frequently by (all, or urban, or rural) children in the group was ＿＿.

All materials given out were well liked by the children, but the urban children actually spent more time reading comic books, which they got from their home environment or by trading with each other.

The illustrations in the (chart or book) entitled ＿＿ excited more spontaneous comments and questions than those in any other; the children's frequent reactions included such phrases as ＿＿, ＿＿, ＿＿.

From the point of view of the teachers, group leaders or parents, the book(s) used most successfully for discussion purposes was (were) ＿＿.

Within the non-fiction category, the titles the children read most were ＿＿, ＿＿, ＿＿.

Conclusions should be based on comments the children make verbally and in writing, some spontaneously and others solicited by the teachers, group leaders, parents. If possible the same materials should be tried out in all types of educational settings.

The materials used in the testing should be made readily available to authors, illustrators, editors and those using literature with children. In this way, they can study the results while examining each specific book (or other item) to determine what appealed (or did not appeal) to children.

WRITING

In the least developed nations, all too often, the most basic materials and services are not available to future writers. Small testing centres, such as those mentioned above, should have modest funds available for writers who wish to test out their writing: for instance, to pay for manuscript paper, or to make sufficient photocopies of manuscripts so that the testing can be carried out or to provide copies to committee members in a government ministry for the 'approval' process.

Training courses for writers can be improved by the use of better model collections for prospective writers to study, which may be obtained, in part, by translating material from other languages. For example, the numerous revisions of a manuscript by a good international children's writer could be reproduced in sequence, showing the stages up to the final printed book, to demonstrate the author's step-by-step efforts to achieve just the right language. Too many authors in too many countries write for children with the mistaken idea that it is easy. They are offended if their work is edited or cut, when in reality their writing lacks clarity or is too adult in concept or point of view to interest children.

Some of the best examples from transcribed oral literature of other countries should also be made widely available, together with the printed versions as they appeared in successfully published children's literature. There are good examples of this craft in a number of languages. Writers need to study from the best examples of folk literature the methods of selecting the story elements that transfer well from oral to printed form. They need to see how language must change and expand or contract when one does not have the voices and gestures of the story-teller to give life to the tale.

International agencies might help in assembling these 'model collections' and in translating the appropriate materials into local languages. These collections should be accompanied by self-teaching guides so that each item may be understood and found helpful, without the direction of a full-time instructor.

Textbook writers should also have access to the above type of collection. Much more time should be spent in training textbook writers who can produce material that is of interest and use in non-formal as well as formal education. They should be encouraged to include local oral literature devices that are known to be popular with children and that are almost never found in textbooks, e.g. riddles, folk-rhymes, chants, songs, tongue-twisters, jokes, etc. Education departments should encourage teachers to collect such oral material overheard among children at play, and to send it in to a central collection point where the oral language and folklore of children can be studied to determine how their language patterns do or do not change.

Larger study collections should be developed for countries that are slightly more advanced in production. International organizations might also develop and supply these collections, supplementing them on a regular annual basis. Such study collections should be housed where they are likely to get the most use, but an ideal location would include a site where children can be observed in their spontaneous response to the literature.

Modest funds should be made available to local writers to pay for their time spent in translating some of the appropriate models in the basic collections. Often, writers can learn a great deal in this translating process.

ILLUSTRATING

In the least developed nations, using items from the collections mentioned above, illustrators can be given models of the kind of pre-school materials that are commonly used to prepare children for literacy, e.g. alphabet and counting books; books or charts that teach basic concepts of colour, shape, size and texture; materials that exemplify individual and societal values that the country wishes to stress. If there are no known illustrators or artists, a modest competition could be held in which each interested person would submit a series of illustrations

Made to measure: children's books in developing countries

telling, in purely pictorial form, a story based on a local folk-tale, or depicting local objects known by name by every child.

A selected number of illustrators might be given stipends for a year to study models, produce prototypes and participate in the testing of pictorial materials for young children. Care should be taken to test the materials among literate and non-literate parents, in formal and non-formal situations. Materials should be tested comparatively, e.g. more than one alphabet book or chart should be designed and tried out with the same groups. The prototypes could be all in rough, original form, or with outlines printed by mechanical means and then filled in with hand-colouring, much as plates used to be made in earlier days in Europe. No colour printing should be done until the illustrators have had quite a wide experience in hand-producing prototype materials.

Courses for illustrators should emphasize hand production of books and materials, through screen processes, block printing and the like. They should also emphasize the basic skills of making story-boards, dummies, hand-made colour separations, and hand-lettered texts.

Textbook illustrators can be taught to broaden their skills to make textbooks more appealing and readable through effective design and illustration. They may be given models of illustration that show the importance of depicting all types of local children in their books. Far too many textbooks show children of only one social class or group. Courses and workshops could be organized to explore how to make the materials more appealing and self-explanatory and usable by parents who cannot afford to send their children to school. This is especially crucial in areas where a large proportion of children is still not able to attend school regularly.

In countries with somewhat more experience in children's book production, illustrators with demonstrated talent could be given the opportunity to spend time in advanced study in one or more of the children's book publishing centres of Europe,

Asia, or North America. Regular exchanges on a three- or six-month basis could be arranged for one or two illustrators each year. Publishers from developed countries should be encouraged to consider the work of these illustrators for publication, especially in connection with illustrated folklore from developing countries.

EDITING

In the least developed nations, editing skills have to be taught, perhaps by short- or long-term experts contracted for this purpose. In this case, care should be taken to match the needs of the country with the background and language skills of the expert. In small countries where first publishing efforts for children are likely to be limited, an outside expert should have, if possible, editing skills combined with a knowledge of graphic design and printing, so that the local counterparts can see demonstrated all the aspects involved in creating children's materials.

Above all, writers and illustrators must be aware that criticism is a necessary part of the process of preparing manuscripts for final publication and that it may all too often be overlooked in children's materials. This will help to discourage vanity publishing, which rarely serves the needs of children. Also, it will give children in developing countries the same high quality in their locally produced publications that they see in imported ones. This is vital if they are to identify their own culture with quality materials; otherwise they will grow up thinking that their local products are always inferior.

Editing textbooks and supplementary materials may also in certain situations benefit from outside expertise. Emphasis should be given to developing skills that will enable local persons to select the most appropriate and appealing texts from oral folklore, so as to incorporate them into literature and reading materials and free them from the constraints that are often found in textbooks.

In more advanced publishing countries, centres can be set up where prospective authors and illustrators can receive the constructive criticism of an objective editor, even though there is no likehood of publication of the material. Editors-in-training might be given the opportunity to spend one or two months abroad, so as to extend their skills and enlarge their professional experience.

Publishers should recognize the special editing skills needed to produce children's materials of quality, and should have the appropriate positions in their publishing firms, giving adequate salaries. Editing is, perhaps, the single most deficient area in creating and publishing children's books in developing countries.

DESIGN

As in the case of editing, skill in design may have to depend on outside expertise at first in the least developed nations. However, it should not be overlooked. Book design determines readability, appeal and many other factors affecting the child reader, and is all too often given short shrift.

A few basic research projects should be undertaken to help determine some of the aspects of design that make inexpensive books appealing and readable for children in developing countries. Virtually all the research done so far has dealt with children in technologically advanced countries, or with design of such subject materials as health posters and charts or materials designed for teaching literacy. No study could be found documenting responses of children in developing countries to the design and layout of story materials. When separate design elements, such as colour, type size, or illustration style, have been tested, this has invariably been done by taking apart these elements and showing them piecemeal to children, rather than by considering them as part of an intrinsic whole, and testing comparatively by using the entire range of design factors. This is especially important for materials that are meant to serve both as school texts and recreational reading.

In countries with expanding production, authorities may wish to consider special prizes or citations for the best-designed books. Design courses related to children's materials should be added to courses preparing students for the printing and publishing industries.

PUBLISHING

Countries in the early stages of publishing for children should examine all the facets of state and private publishing, so as to determine which type suits the country best or whether a mix of both is the most effective solution. In any case, subsidies may have to come chiefly from public funds, since it is unlikely that private purchasing power will be sufficient to support the development of children's materials. Virtually all countries in the world, with the possible exception of Japan, find that they must publicly support a high proportion of the production of children's materials, either by direct subsidy, or by indirect means (e.g. purchase of large amounts of material through the use of public funds, enabling print runs that are large and economical enough to allow for private purchase as well).

To complement local publishing, co-publishing should be attempted among groups of countries and among different language publishers in the same country. A model worth studying is the Asian Co-publication Programme sponsored by the Asian Cultural Centre for Unesco in Tokyo. Co-publishing could be considered on a bilateral or multilateral basis, government to government or publisher to publisher.

Publishers of school text materials should attempt to develop this type so as to reach the out-of-school child. This will often mean redesigning the materials, sometimes even total rewriting. There is a tendency for text publishers to become complacent and unwilling to change, since in their view the materials will be bought anyway, once they are on an approved list. Care must be taken, when setting up, expanding or changing the system of textbook publishing, that controls exist so as to encourage the publishers to act in the best interests of the child, and not merely in the fashion most expedient for themselves.

Policy-makers should examine whether it is more efficient (and results in better materials for children) to subsidize all textbooks and supplementary materials by one body, or whether it is better to separate the two. Educational authorities might be encouraged to consider the use of non-textbook material in formal schooling to determine whether children are better served by a choice of materials.

Books published in another country but suited to local use could be considered in order to give children the full range of materials necessary for the kind of broad education we would like them to have. This is especially true for countries using the same or similar languages. The Nordic countries are a good example of highly industrialized nations sharing a great deal of each other's published materials for children, partly because the economics of printing in all the languages would be prohibitive in relation to the number of users, and partly to have their children grow up with a deeper understanding of the subtle differences that exist among their neighbouring countries.

Language differences from country to country can cause confusion in children but, if used positively, can also bring about greater empathy and understanding. National publishers in both developed and developing countries should be encouraged to share materials for their mutual benefit.

DISTRIBUTION

In the least developed nations, book distribution mechanisms should take maximum advantage of existing systems of distribution of goods and services. All too often, separate distribution patterns are followed by each ministry in any given country, even though all are attempting to reach the same children, and none are truly effective. Very few attempts have been made to 'piggy-back' educational or recreational materials on to delivery of essential services. For example, in cases where regular delivery of postal or health services to small centres occurs, it should be possible to include a certain amount of visual and reading material meant for regular posting on the walls of such centres, or for reading use in the waiting areas. Auxiliaries or volunteers could be trained in simple story-telling techniques. This would keep both mothers and children happily occupied during the long waiting periods at clinics and health centres.

These materials should be as pleasurable for parents as they are for children, and should be easy to read even by new literates. They should not be overloaded with heavy messages, but be fun to read and look at. They should be issued with some regularity, and in an easily recognizable form, so that the impetus to continue reading to the children will come spontaneously, without the outside urging of a specialist or educator.

Studies should be undertaken to determine alternative methods for textbook effectiveness and distribution. At present, it is customary in most developing countries for pupils to purchase their textbooks outright, or, in a few cases, for the government to give them free. In either case, the schools rarely keep complete class sets of textbooks, as is common in North America and in some European countries.

Since textbooks are rarely read for pleasure and most are not too useful in self-instructional contexts, it would be wise to examine the extent and method of distribution to see if more children could be served by the same number of textbooks. Comparative projects might be funded in a few countries, in which textbook sets with somewhat heavier bindings could be deposited for two or three years in one group of schools in sufficient quantities to enable all children to have them for use when needed, but not to keep. In another group of schools, the children would be given each year less expensive paper-covered versions of the same textbooks and would be allowed to take them home permanently at the end of the school term. Periodic visits to the families of randomly selected children could then be made, to observe and document out-of-school use of the textbooks, if any, and the difference in use between school-owned or child-owned textbooks.

Countries dispensing free text materials might wish to consider forms that are less expensive and more effective when distributed on a weekly or monthly basis. For example, an inexpensive newsprint-style, four-page 'reader' or mathematics and science booklet, printed at different grade levels and in sufficient quantities to hand out free to each child on a weekly basis, might well prove more effective and less costly in the end than a set of 100-page textbooks distributed at the beginning of each year. There might also be more flexibility in such materials and more appeal to the out-of-school child. For tropical areas where books do not wear well unless they are very expensively produced, this 'disposable' type of textbook might be more economical in the end.

On the other hand, some countries might find it more economical to print on very high quality paper and with strong bindings, and aim for distribution once every ten years, with the schools keeping the materials from year to year and using them with each new class of children. New methods of distribution should be tried out, especially on a long-term basis, so that such experiences can be documented and costed for reference use by other countries. Only then will there be incentives to experiment with other methods, rather than maintaining outdated, ineffective distribution systems.

Where larger and more varied production prevails, sales methods for bookstalls and stores can be improved, but more important, the 'basic appeal' of the materials must be enhanced. The appeal in such cases must be principally to the adult in the family who is buying for children. A sizeable number of families are moving up to the ranks of those who can afford to buy pleasure articles for their children. Often, they buy things that have no lasting value and may occasionally be harmful. It is important for these families to realize that it is possible to buy articles that give pleasure and, at the same time, stimulate their children's intellectual and social growth. Television and radio, where they exist, should be utilized in more dramatic ways to create interest in good reading materials for children. This can be done through outright advertising, but a better method is to have dramatic episodes from children's literature presented skilfully on these media, followed by announcements of availability of the books or other materials, and stressing the importance of giving this kind of reading matter to children.

Book clubs selling inexpensive paperback versions of children's literature of proven popularity could be set up to function in all schools. More campaigns should be launched to impress upon parents the importance of giving intellectual nutrition and 'sweets', if they wish their children to become lifetime readers. In these efforts, parents should be reminded that it is necessary to talk or sing to their babies, in rhyme and in prose. They should also be shown how easy it is for parents to prepare their children for reading and writing by pointing out pictures of things, by calling attention to letters or words on signs or labels, and by giving their children chalk, crayons, pencils, or even small sticks, and letting them scribble 'pictures' in the dirt or on some sort of surface. Simple booklets or flyers could be wrapped around basic items sold for child care.

PROMOTION

As mentioned above, in the least developed nations parents must be convinced that it is still important to tell or read stories to children, from a very early age. These oral methods, which were so prevalent in most societies, are now often dying out. In addition, parents must be shown the importance of the new kinds of preparation needed for children entering formal systems of schooling. This includes the use of pencil-like objects (so as to prepare for writing); identifying and naming objects in their printed and pictorial representations; learning pictorial, linear sequence that can then be transferred to word sequence; learning that a symbol or letter stands for a sound, etc. Many of these skills can be practised with pre-school children, even by non-literate parents, if they are given the requisite materials, and one clear demonstration. Demonstration could be accomplished by para-professionals live or via radio (or television where it is commonly available), at health centres, post offices, day-care centres, military installations, community centres, factories, work sites and other places.

The materials must be exceptionally well-designed and appealing, so that both parents and children are attracted to them. Ponderous, didactic language should be avoided. The language should be simple, direct, and in a widely understood vernacular. Rhyme, rhythm and humour should also be used, especially when they are a natural part of the playful uses of language in a particular culture. Generally speaking, a disproportionately high percentage of funding is allocated to production costs such as paper, inks, bindings, etc., and only a small amount is earmarked for content, design and testing of the materials.

International agencies, in co-operation with organizations and individual experts, might assist in developing simple pamphlets, posters, charts, radio and television announcements and the like, showing how such promotion campaigns could be mounted.

Government departments responsible for formal pre-school centres should include in their basic standards for space and equipment a small box or case of books, at least one book for every ten children served. If there are no locally produced pre-school books, the staff could be assisted in developing hand-made books, until a modest local production can get under way. Funds could be set aside expressly for the purpose of locally producing material for these centres, and international agencies could be requested to provide for short-term outside experts, where necessary.

Textbooks should be tried out in non-formal situations, as has been mentioned before. It may be some time before many of the least developed nations can afford to have books for all children on all subjects of interest to them. Therefore, every book must be designed for the widest possible appeal and use, and not the narrowest. In training and retraining of teachers, the use of oral literature should be emphasized, along with that of printed literature. Teachers should be given the opportunity to see that entertaining and inspiring reading materials often foster longer lasting reading habits and skills in children than do materials of a pedestrian, overly didactic nature.

Simple course outlines in story-telling, oral folklore and written children's literature could be designed. These could be incorporated gradually into the curricula of all teacher-training institutions. The courses should include the study of some children's materials from other countries, and could therefore be accompanied by small study collections.

Library systems are a major means of supplying children with books and other reading materials. Public and school libraries, home libraries, book-box schemes, mobile libraries, cultural centres and the like all have an important role to play in serving even the remotest regions.

At present, there are almost no comparative data on start-up costs, maintenance costs, and relative effectiveness of the various types of library techniques in developing countries. For example, some countries have begun expensive and long-range plans for the development of school libraries, but without testing whether the formal school systems and staff are sufficiently adaptable to absorb this new component, or whether other systems would be more appropriate. Often, the formal school is the place least able to adapt to new techniques and materials. In such cases, the same staff time and funds might go further and reach more children more effectively if they were expended for library activities in community, health, or cultural centres, or any other well-run public facilities. Once certain library materials and techniques are demonstrated as effective, the schools might then be more ready to incorporate them into the curricula, and school libraries can then become the key centres of learning that they should be.

Rotating book boxes and home library schemes would appear to be very adaptable to a number of developing countries and could serve as an effective complement to fixed school or public libraries in getting reading materials to children.

Greater public-relations efforts must be directed towards children to show the prestige and pleasure attached to owning books. For example, some governments might find it effective to reward perfect attendance, high marks, and other similar achievements among schoolchildren with gifts of well-produced, attractive books at the end of the academic year. Such automatic subsidy would provide incentive to publishers to produce high-quality materials, and at the same time would enhance the average child's desire to own books. The contents could be beautifully illustrated plates of local birds, animals, plants, flowers, etc., accurately described at the child's level. Books of this type are very costly to produce, but in large print runs become less costly per volume. They also are a very necessary tool for teaching respect for the environment.

Locally printed children's literature should also be available on films, filmstrips, radio and television, when such media exist. Many countries have found through experience that children respond very well to the same material in different forms. Rather than hindering reading, this tends to reinforce it.

Bibliography

Included in this bibliography are all items mentioned in the text, and other materials that support the statements or theories I have formulated. I have also included a few practical books that might be helpful to those involved in creating and producing children's books in developing countries. I have not included basic histories, critical works, or anthologies of children's literature, nor any of the many fine journals dealing with the review and criticism of children's literature. Lists for these can easily be obtained from various national sections of the International Board on Books for Young People (IBBY); they are kept up to date by notices of new items in Bookbird magazine. There are also many other books and pamphlets available on the art or craft of writing for children. These may very well be helpful to writers in developing countries, but it seemed better to stress here the need for providing suggestions based on experience and actual practice in developing countries.

ALBORNOZ, Hugo. *Los libros de texto de las escuelas primarias de America*. Washington, D.C., Panamericana, 1964. 60 p.

AMSDEN, R. H. Children's Preferences in Picture Story Book Variables. *Journal of Educational Research*, Vol. 53, 1960, p. 309–12.

Asian Book Development Newsletter. Tokyo, Asian Cultural Centre for Unesco. Quarterly. Vol. 1, No. 1, 1969–. (Earlier title: *Tokyo Book Development Center Newsletter*.)

BADER, Barbara. *American Picturebooks from Noah's Ark to the Beast Within*. New York, Macmillan, 1976. 615 p., bibliogr., ill.

BAMBERGER, Florence Eilau. The Effect of the Physical Make-up of a Book Upon Children's Selection. *Johns Hopkins University Studies in Education* (Baltimore), No. 4, 1922.

BARTO, Agnia. The Training of Specialists for the Production of Books for Children in Russia. *Bookbird* (Dortmund), Vol. 13, No. 1, 1975, p. 10–66.

BIAS, Elizabeth Browning. *The Effect of New Techniques in Printing and Designing on Illustration and Format of Children's Books.* Chapel Hill, 1960. 86 p. Thesis, MSLS.

Bookbird. Quarterly of the International Board on Books for Young People (IBBY), edited in Vienna. (There are numerous articles scattered throughout the past issues of this journal, related to children's books in developed and developing countries.)

BUTLER, Dorothy. *Cushla and Her Books.* London, Hodder and Stoughton, 1979.

CLAY, Marie M. *Reading: the Patterning of Complex Behavior.* London, Heinemann, 1977. 168 p.

Communicating with Pictures. Katmandu, National Development Service and Unicef, 1977.

CRAGO, Hugh; CRAGO, Maureen. The Untrained Eye? A Preschool Child Explores Felix Hoffmann's Rapunzel. *Children's Literature in Education,* No. 22, Autumn 1976.

HALBEY, Hans A. Artistic Quality in the Children's Book. *Graphis* (Zürich), Vol. 20, No. 3, 1964, p. 30–51.

HILDICK, Edmund Wallace. *Children and Fiction: a Critical Study in Depth of the Artistic and Psychological Factors Involved in Writing Fiction for and about Children.* London, Evans Bros., 1970. 204 p.

KLITGAARD, S. A. *Educational Books in West, Central and East Africa.* London, George G. Harrap (in co-operation with Unesco), 1967. 74 p.

MARTIN, Helen. Children's Preferences in Book Illustration. *Western Reserve University Bulletin* (Cleveland), Vol. 34 (new series), No. 10, 15 July 1931, p. 1–58.

MELCHING, Molly. Meeting Children on Their Own Terms in Senegal. *Wilson Library Bulletin,* Vol. 54, No. 2, October 1979, p. 109–11.

Newsletter, Unesco Regional Office for Culture and Book Development in Asia (Karachi). Quarterly. Vol. 1, No. 1, April 1959–. (Original title: *Information Bulletin on Reading Materials.*)

NKWOCHA, Philip U. Publishing for Children. In: *Publishing in Nigeria,* p. 39–43. Benin City, Ethiope Pub. Corp., 1972.

PELLOWSKI, Anne. *The World of Children's Literature.* New York, R. R. Bowker, 1968. 538 p.

——. *The World of Storytelling.* New York, R. R. Bowker, 1977. 296 p.

PEÑALOSA, Fernando. *The Mexican Book Industry*. New York, Scarecrow, 1957.

[Picture Books.] *China Monthly Review*, April 1952.

PLUMB, David J. *Design and Print Production Workbook*. Middlesex, Workbook Publications, 1978. 46 p.

Putting the Book in Hand, Including Preparation Up to Composition. London, British Printing Industries Federation/Publishers' Association, 1975. 24 p.

RICE, Stanley. *Book Design: Systematic Aspects; Text Format Models*. New York, R. R. Bowker Co., 1978. 256 p.

SMERDON, Gerald. Children's Preferences in Illustration. *Children's Literature in Education*, No. 20, Spring 1976.

SULLIVAN, George. *A Reason to Read: A Report on an International Symposium on the Promotion of the Reading Habit*. Sponsored by the United States National Commission for Unesco, 5-8 May 1976. New York, Academy for Educational Development, 1976. 109 p., bibliogr.

Survey of School Textbooks in India, 1969-1970. New Delhi, National Council of Educational Research and Training, 1971.

TAUBERT, Sigfred. *Bibliopola, Pictures and Texts about the Book Trade*. Hamburg, Ernst Hauswedell & Co., 1966. 2 vols. (Text in German, English, French.)

VAN HORNE, Marion. *Give Children Wings; A Manual on How to Write for Children*. New York, Committee on World Literacy and Christian Literature, 1970. 109 p.

WATTS, Lynne; NISBET, John. *Legibility in Children's Books: A Review of Research*. Windsor, United Kingdom, NFER, 1974.

WHALLEY, Joyce Irene. *Cobwebs to Catch Flies; Illustrated Books for the Nursery and Schoolroom 1700-1900*. Berkeley and Los Angeles, University of California Press, 1975.

ZIMET, Sara Goodman et al. Attitudes and Values in Primers from the United States and Twelve Other Countries. *What Children Read in School; Critical Analysis of Primary Reading Textbooks*, p. 99-114. New York and London, Grune & Stratton, 1972. Also in *Journal of Social Psychology*, Vol. 84, 1971, p. 167-74.